Homo Northwestus

A Quest for the Species, North-West Man

Based on the Granada Television series with Ray Gosling

written by Bill Jones, with Liz Andrew

with photographs by Ian Beesley

Carnegie Publishing, 1992

Homo Northwestus

A quest for the species, North-West Man

written by Bill Jones, with Liz Andrew

Text copyright © Granada Television Ltd., 1992

Published by Carnegie Publishing Ltd., 18 Maynard Street, Preston.

First edition, March 1992

Designed and typeset in 10½/14 Times Roman by Carnegie Publishing.
Printed and bound in the UK by The Bath Press, Bath.

British Library Cataloguing-in-Publication Data
A CIP catalogue record for this book is available from the British Library

ISBN 0-948789-81-6

Contents

Ray Gosling has been a writer and broadcaster for nearly three decades. An ex-teddy boy, he wrote his first book, an autobiography, while still in his teens. His recent television credits include *Class by Class* for Channel 4 and *The Forgotten Front* for Granada Television.

Bill Jones has worked at Granada Television for ten years. Before that he worked on newspapers in Bolton and York. Before that he went to Lancaster University. Before that he remembers very little although his mother tells him he was born in Yorkshire. His private passions are Mozart, the Cuillins of Skye and three people called Kay, Alex and Sam.

Like Homo Northwestus, Liz Andrew is a mongrel. Although she was born in Blackpool, her parents were of Scots-Irish descent. She read English at Oxford. The television programmes she has worked for include *End of Empire*, *Victorian Values* and *Disappearing World*. No longer in Blackpool,she enjoys a home in the remoter wilds of South Cumbria where she is frequently taken for long walks by her dog Towser.

Ian Beesley is one of Britain's leading independent photographers. His work has been exhibited at the National Museum of Photography, Bradford, and the Photographers' Gallery, London, and is included in various national collections.

Acknowledgements

F ROM the first idea to the final edit took exactly one year. Although, in the beginning it was just one person, the team was gradually swollen by the names which appear below. In turn, each became absorbed by our quest for Homo Northwestus. From the outset it was acknowledged that we might not find him, but everyone knew they would enjoy the search. It is thanks to these people that Homo Northwestus is as much fun to watch as it was to make: research: Liz Andrew, Ros Wyatt, Alice Cooper; production co-ordinator: Lesley Haselum; production assistant: Tina Kirk; graphic design: Carole Ricketts, A4 Animation, Bristol; film editors: Leo Kretscher, Eddie Mansell; assistant film editors: Kath Jones, Steve Kretscher; lighting: Pete Smith, Graham Heyes; sound: Phil Taylor, Ray French; photography: Lawrence Jones, Gorden McGregor, Nick Plowright; executive producer: Stuart Prebble; editor: Charles Tremayne; directors: Charles Kitchen, Tony Bulley.

The series and the book would also have been impossible without the help of: Marion Hewitt at the North West Film Archive; Clive Garner; Bob Dobson; The Corner Pin, Stubbins; the Queen Street Mill, Burnley; the East Lancashire Railway Co.; National Children's Homes; King Arthur and his knights at the Camelot theme park; The Irish Centre, Cheetham Hill, Manchester; the Lancashire and Cheshire Federation of Scottish Societies; Alan Bell and the Fylde Folk Festival; Uncle Joe's Mint Balls; Manchester United Football Club; Keith Clifford, the Frank Randle impersonator; Mike Blakeley; Towneley Hall, Burnley; The Beatles Centre, Liverpool; the Lord Daresbury Hotel, Cheshire; Museum of Childhood, Ribchester; the priory and castle of the City of Lancaster; the Trinity Court Development, Manchester; Casdons of Blackpool; British Rail; Megabowl; Eileen Bilton; Wigan Rugby League Club; the Hodder Valley Show committee . . . together with all those members of the tribe who feature or who are interviewed in the six film documentaries.

Bill Jones
Producer, *Homo Northwestus*
March, 1992

SUDDENLY, it seems as if everyone is in pursuit of their identity. Not just a family tree, but deeper roots. Roots which throughout Europe have survived some awful times. In Yugoslavia, the Croats; in Spain, the Basques; and in Russia, forgotten states, sleeping species of whole peoples, put names to their patches and said, 'This is us, let us choose, let us govern ourselves, we are different'.

I wondered, how far could it go?

How easy it has been to see how English people feel apart from continental Europeans. Many, perhaps most, of us may want to be closer – it makes sense – but does that make it feel right? Our sense of belonging to these islands runs so deep. Is it an instinct; an old, tribal xenophobic fear? Is it something we can't change? We'd bashed back the Armada; turned away Napoleon at Fishguard; the white cliffs of Dover had made Hitler blink and retreat. It takes an effort sometimes to understand why we should share a common currency when our culture is so different, our isolation so old.

English people behave differently, too; are more stoical, less passionate (it is said) than others. Colder, maybe, as a consequence of being so stuck out in the North Sea. And if there are characteristics which we can say are English, or Welsh, or Ukranian, is that as far as we can go? Can a smaller region, or a town, have an identity which has evolved and to which people feel attached, sometimes without their even knowing it? Or in Britain, where people move about so much, are we all becoming the same?

Not so. Certainly not so in Central Southern England where there was an outcry when the Meteorological Office summarily abolished it for the purposes of BBC weather forecasts. 'Nobody really knew where it was,' said Barry Parker of the Met. Office. But they did. In Cirencester and Poole, Southampton and Stratford, the residents took to their pens, pointing out that their weather had little in common with Kent or Cornwall. And now, if you listen, Central Southern England has been restored to the map, its rainfall gleefully chronicled on every bulletin. In fact, some would say the Central Southerners now get rather more than their fair share of weather.

So what of the North-West? What idiosyncratic peculiarities set its people apart, make it unique, a nation unto itself? Where do its people come from? What do others see when they look at this rough-hewn northern species?

Throughout the world there are people who think they know the answers: a race of George Formbys, they'll say, forever clip-clopping to work in the shadow of a gigantic flat cap. That is what so many expect. And, yet, how much of that is true of the people of the North-West? And are we in any sense a species as proud and alone as a Latvian, a Croat, a Basque? What price independence for Homo Northwestus, our North-West Man?

△ Is George Formby really the archetypical Homo Northwestus? Or is he just a cardboard cut-out conveniently created by southern image-makers? Surely we need to look elsewhere for the true nature and character of Homo Northwestus . . .

Homo Northwestus. The title had caused long discussion and endless agonising. Not everyone on the production team had liked it, and yet the alternatives all gave the impression that these were history films, which they were not. They were to be more like essays, really – very quizzical – and Homo Northwestus became the fictitious identikit picture we would build. His features would be those identifying marks which only North-West people have. And even if (as we expected) it proved impossible to unite us all as one species, perhaps by accident we might speed the process of evolution; awaken a truly proud, self-conscious northern race, west of the Pennine backbone.

Certainly it was happening elsewhere. Essex Man was born in Wapping, where Essex jokes and tabloid tales mapped out a species which travelled in XR3i cars, carving out dubious deals on mobile phones. And in Austria, too, where the frozen corpse of a Bronze Age farmer was prised loose from a crumbling glacier and christened *homo tirolensis*, Tirol Man. As if Central Southern England wasn't enough, suddenly everyone was clubbing and clanning together. From Moldavia to Macclesfield, strange new voices began chattering and chuntering for home rule and regional government and . . . are we really so different in anything but our accents, perhaps, or the view from our windows? In his heart, is a Geordie so far removed from a Taffy, or a Mick, or a Lanky lad?

In an age when universal franchises stretch around the world, when McDonald's will welcome you to Moscow and Merseyside with the self-same outstretched Big Mac, it seemed worth trying to find out. Because if it turned out that there were lingering traces of those special things which set Lancashire apart, someone might do more than build an industrial theme park. They might look up a neighbour, perhaps? Or fight for a footpath on a Peak bog?

The bog, after all, is where Homo Northwestus had spent so much of his time . . . even since time began . . .

Ray Gosling

▽ Tracing the origins of the species leads one to the most surprising locations . . . Here intrepid broadcaster Ray Gosling finds inspiration in the shed of an allotment in Preston. But what about that pig, Ray?

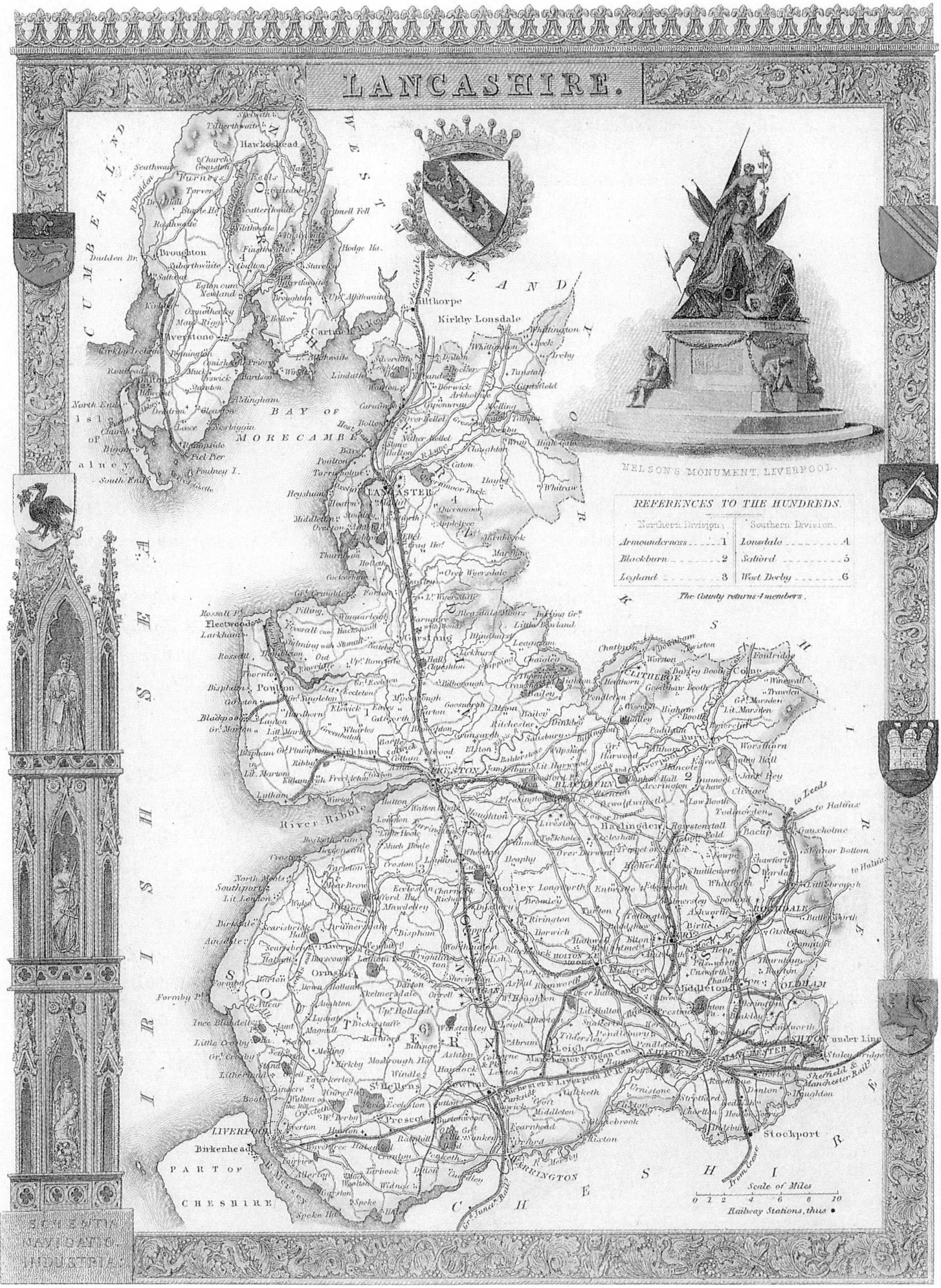

LANCASHIRE.

NELSON'S MONUMENT, LIVERPOOL.

REFERENCES TO THE HUNDREDS.

Northern Division		Southern Division	
Armounderness	1	Lonsdale	4
Blackburn	2	Salford	5
Leyland	3	West Derby	6

The County returns 4 members.

Scale of Miles

Railway Stations, thus ●

SCIENTIA NAVIGANDO INDUSTRIA

CUMBERLAND

WESTMORELAND

BAY OF MORECAMBE

IRISH SEA

YORKSHIRE

PART OF CHESHIRE

LANCASTER

PRESTON

BLACKBURN

BOLTON

LIVERPOOL

Birkenhead

Stockport

Southport

Ormskirk

Fleetwood

Hawkshead

Kirkby Lonsdale

Garstang

Clitheroe

Colne

Burnley

Haslingden

Rochdale

Oldham

Middleton

Bury

St Helens

Prescot

Warrington

Widnes

Speke

| Chapter ONE | # 38 out of 38 |

E VERYONE wants to belong; to know who they are and where they're from; and that they're wanted. Often it's without thinking, but how often do we go away and miss home, feeling strongly different in a foreign place? In Turkey or Torremolinos we can feel more powerfully part of a tribe than ever we can in Todmorden or Tarporley, and to feel you were 'Lancashire' used to mean something very special. It was much more than a name on a passport, or a scarf round your neck which says 'Wigan'. More than a football shirt, or a pop group from Manchester.

From Blundellsands to Blackburn, from Barrow to Daisy Nook, folk would say, 'The Red Rose is my home,' and that family which is Lancashire had an image which travelled the world. Warm-hearted, industrious, straight-talking, stubborn. And round the tight contours of the map you could see how much geographical sense this North-West made. From the north-facing mountains of Merioneth, you could trace a line across the tops, round the Cheshire plains to the Pennines, then right up the backbone of England to the Lake District. Here was a self-sufficient tribe; independent; almost its own state with border posts at Bangor, Macclesfield, Bacup and Kendal. Everything on that west side between the hills and the Irish Sea was the kingdom of Lancashire; and its king, of course, was cotton.

But, as much as the geography of the place made sense, did it breed a North-West Man; some sort of Homo Northwestus? Was there then – is there now – a breed apart, a tribe we might acknowledge?

Local pride certainly used to be so important, and where you

◁ The old county of Lancashire was a backward place until the coming of industry at the end of the eighteenth century. Thomas Moule said in his notes to this 1830s' map, 'Lancashire is divided into 6 hundreds, which contain 27 market towns, 62 parishes, and 894 villages . . . and extensive bogs or mosses', but added that 'as a commercial and manufacturing county, Lancashire is distinguished beyond most others in the kingdom.'

came from made you. All Lancashire – not just Wigan pie-eaters – felt itself to be a special breed: wittier, less pompous than Yorkshire. More natural, at ease, and better off for being worse off than the dreadful South of England.

And Lancashire had been so proud. Liverpool was Lancashire; Manchester, too; and the cotton towns, the coal towns, the chemical towns. Warrington and Preston were Lancashire. All of it so big and bustling and, beyond its borders, the colonies annexed and conquered by the chieftains of this new industrial species. It was Manchester money which built villas alongside Lake Windermere, and flooded Thirlmere so that city people could drink its water seventy miles to the south. It was Dr. Mould of Cheadle who built Colwyn Bay. The Platts of Oldham were behind Llanfairfechan and, at Dwygyfylchi, it was Samuel Duckinfield Derbyshire whose influence built a sea-bathing resort and changed its name to Penmaenmawr for ease of pronunciation.

South Cumbria, North Wales, Derbyshire and Cheshire: each was grafted on to the tribal homeland of Lancashire, from where Homo Northwestus could travel to Alderley Edge by electric train, and to the better parts of Birkenhead by steam ferry. And although Lancashire towns could have their squabbles (Bolton and Bury, Oldham and Rochdale), we could unite for more than just cricket. All Cheshire came in with Lancashire when it mattered, against the South of England, or Yorkshire people. It was said that Lancashire people then, even quite recently, were one species, a tribe – Homo Northwestus – who could all share the same scarf. But is the same true now?

People flit about so much – for work, for their holidays all over the world – it's sometimes hard to see what local loyalty can count for any more. As more of us get better off, and old patterns of work fade, the industrial towns become feeder suburbs populated by transients; outsiders who have come from somewhere else only to discover that they like it here and want to stay. It's impossible, as this happens, to see how the old community ties can linger on. And yet, for some people, in some places, it's as keenly felt as it ever was. In Southport, for instance.

The gentry who first discovered these Ribble dunes would be surprised, and then charmed, by the Southport of today. It had been little but marram grass until the 1790s, when the rich first

> 6 People flit about so much . . . it's sometimes hard to see what local loyalty can count for any more. 9

△ Exactly two hundred years ago one William Sutton built his 'South Port Hotel' among the sand-dunes of the Lancashire coast. This painting dates from around 1845 and shows how quickly the resort was growing.

came to install their bathing machines on the vast plains of wind-blown sand. They had dipped their toes into the sea from their carefully segregated swimming areas and found the place delightful. So much did it please them that they bought plots from the local lords of the manor (hence Lord Street), and laid the gardens right up to the road.

You could catch a steamer from the pier then. Not until 1923 did the sea complete its retreat, beaching the boats which ferried trippers from Southport to Barrow, North Wales, Liverpool and beyond to the Isle of Man. Southport was a polite, proper place, a Harrogate-by-the-Sea, from which Club trains whisked a new class of commuting tycoons to their desks in Bold Street or St. Anne's Square. In and out of its tea rooms, along the bushy boulevards and wrought-iron arcades, the town acquired an identity, a reputation, to which its populace was proudly attached. Not mucky Lancashire, but Lancashire just the same, and as surely so as Ramsbottom or Preston. And then, suddenly, they were moved. Not a brick had turned in its bed of mortar, but all of Southport had rolled overnight into a new land, and her name was 'Merseyside'.

It was Ted Heath who'd bulldozed the old boundaries, and throughout the country there were people who didn't like it. To Grimsby was joined Bridlington, but no longer in the East Riding: now it was Humberside, North and South. Into Cumbria went Ulverston, and out of Lancashire went cities and towns:

Manchester and Liverpool, Salford and Southport – where people howled. All along leafy Lord Street the descendants of those first bathing gentry rose up, sending over *ten thousand* letters of complaint, demanding to be let back in, set free from this 'Merseyside' many felt appalled by.

But not everyone was unhappy. Although most people felt their heritage had been betrayed, there were some who quietly smiled at being let off so lightly. Like Warrington, whose admittance into the 'Cheshire set' lined it up with Wilmslow, making their New Town a much more desirable address than it might have been. Others, like many in the East Riding, refused to acknowledge the new metropolitan authorities, and, in letters, remained true to their old address, their old homeland. But nowhere has the battle run on so long as in Southport.

On stickers and leaflets people say 'Join the Fight, Southport out of Merseyside', and the Boundary Commission totters under the weight of their protests. 'What can we possibly have in common with inner-city Bootle, or Litherland?' they say. 'We were our own independent borough,' they say, 'and we liked it the way it was.' No-one ever says (or at least, not on the leaflets) that it's the very *idea* of Merseyside that they resent. Southport may be snooty, but never vocally so. In any case, wasn't Liverpool part of that old Lancashire to which they would like to return?

It's funny how the tiny signs of change often anger Lancashire people the most. In Rochdale bus station they still grieve over the changing of their bus colour from lobelia blue to orange, as in Southport they miss their 'blood and custard'. You ask Tony Harrison, whose quality furniture shop thrives behind the art deco windows of T. R. Highton's arcade on Lord Street: 'Sentimentally, emotionally, I want to be Lancastrian again,' he says in an upstairs showroom cluttered with Parker Knoll chairs. ('*Everybody's* mother has one,' he adds.)

Tony's family has been in the town since 1810 and, for twelve years before the boundary changes, he'd been a Tory councillor. But not any more. Tony didn't want to fall in with Sefton or Merseyside, and thought the new marriage more of a wake than a wedding. 'The whole feel of Southport was as a family, and yet nobody feels a family any more. It's too big. It was all done when bigness mattered, whereas we know now it's totally wrong.'

Poor Tony. Even as his snowy-haired customers come and go he mourns. 'It's never out of my mind,' he muses. 'I still don't like it. I still can't take it, and I hope we go back as soon as possible.'

Back to what? To those old Southport buses? As much as he blames a new régime for a foreign shabbiness in his town, is it not all a fuss about nothing? Or does the colour of the buses signify something much deeper?

It is a funny thing, local loyalty, but the older ones of Lancashire did feel it, and still do. So when Ted Heath waded in, it was felt that their inheritance had been diverted, messed, broken; that their boundaries had been mucked about with more than the Soviet Union's. From London we told them that they belonged to Greater Manchester County, but they truly belonged to Lancashire towns. And as old Lancashire shrank, the idea of a North-West, beyond political lines, began to grow. Network North-West on the railways. *Look North-West* on the television. And, for a brief while, a *North West Times* on our newstands.

And so, in less than two decades, it seems as if the Lancashire that Tony Harrison celebrates has all but faded away, an echo of itself to be enjoyed on day trips to Wigan Pier and the Albert Dock. Although in his heyday Homo Northwestus had stood for something, had set standards in humour and energy, what does he stand for now? Everyone wants to belong – of course they do; but that romantically, powerfully great Lancashire that many hanker after actually existed for little more than a hundred bustling Victorian years. In his rush to market his past, Homo Northwestus has constructed a phoney version of events, almost entirely based on the events of the nineteenth century.

To find out who he is, and what's to become of the species, it might help to know the truth of what Homo Northwestus was *before* the industrial revolution, before clogs and Coronation Street. Because when they were hanging gardens in Babylon there was nowt here. We were bottom of the class.

△ Wigan pit brow girls were a favourite subject for Victorian photographers, giving a romanticised view of what was a terrible job and proving that marketing the past is nothing new . . .

It's in a hideaway wood behind a Little Chef east of Ulverston that Homo Northwestus first pops up; living, it seems, at the edge of a melting icecap and already seeking a quiet retreat from the warmer, busier south (as many retired citizens of nearby Grange-over-Sands still do). He'd found a south-facing limestone cliff, never more than fifteen feet high, and pitted with caves from which he could watch the meltwaters empty their silt into Morecambe Bay. Across his view would drift the Irish elk and arctic foxes he'd feed on, and his traps would fill with Siberian vole and lemmings. Maybe there'd be an arctic-alpine snail *(pyramidula ruderata)* for *hors d'oeuvres* . . .

But it wasn't much cop, life in this limestone forerunner of the terraced street. In his twenties Homo Northwestus was an old man, who'd happily chuck his feeble infants into the back of his cave for archaeologist Chris Salisbury to discover twelve thousand years later. 'They were almost like our first garden sheds,' he says. 'Probably not lived in, but used to store tools and meat and the occasional dead body.'

No art has been found here; nor will it ever be. These were pragmatic people living on the extreme margin of civilisation. Man had first straightened his back on a hot African plain and, in concentric rings, spread slowly north, his prehistoric progress determined by the weather. It was the hot places which developed the fastest. It stands to reason. When in Egypt you could roll up your sleeves to build a sun-kissed pyramid, we were still sticking up stone circles at Swinside in Cumbria – in the rain. Poor people, backward people, and only the toughest, most stubborn of early man must have reached Chris Salisbury's caves. Even then, the South of England was a much more attractive proposition where, in Cheddar Gorge and along the Thames Valley, they wintered up before summer hunting excursions all around Morecambe Bay.

At Lindale and Silverdale, Warton and Humphrey Head, archaeologists have found traces of early Homo Northwestus, and at High Furlong, near Poulton-le-Fylde, they've found the elk that got away. He'd been attacked in winter by hunters armed with bone-tipped spears, only to escape and nurse his leg wounds for a month. A second attack had followed, the spears splintering through his flank and left hind foot. Now the elk could only stagger on. The days were short, and Homo Northwestus gave up the chase. In the gloom, the elk stumbled, sank into a marsh, and was trapped beneath the season's ice, his escape a secret for twelve thousand years . . .

Homo Northwestus was always so out of the

> ❛ It wasn't much cop, life in this limestone forerunner of the terraced street. ❜

▽ Speared by one of the very first Homo Northwesti, this hapless elk fell into a bog – where else? – and was discovered by archaeologists nearly 10,000 years later. We know that it was a victim of a hunter's blade from cut marks on the poor creature's bones.

It seems that Chris Salisbury is very much a case of 'have trowel will travel'. Not just as an archaeologist, either. Until the age of forty he'd spent his entire working life in the building industry. 'I wasn't laying bricks. I was in admin., but I got to that stage in life when you ask, "Why am I chasing the dollar when I could be enjoying myself?" ' So he got out, took a degree, pulled on a pair of robust wellies and delved into the caves and crannies of Morecambe Bay.

▽ Chris Salisbury . . . never happier than up to his armpits in sludge, putting Northern Man back on the prehistoric map.

For back-aching hours he will lie in the glutinous, icy mud of dark, constricted limestone tunnels still choked by the silt of centuries. On a good day he will find, not a gem-encrusted Celtic neckband, but a tooth, a fragment of collar-bone or a crude shard of flint, its edge delicately honed by the earliest of Homo Northwesti. This is not a romantic quest like that of an Egyptologist. Chris will find no Tutankhamun, no gilt-crafted sarcophagus with eyes of the purest lapis lazuli. He's happy enough up to his armpits in sludge, knowing that, through his damp endeavours, Northern Man is being put back on the prehistoric map.

'Before I started exploring around Morecambe Bay people thought the cover of ice was so dense – half a mile thick – there would have been no occupation of the North-West. We've overturned that view. There's real pleasure in that because I'm a Northern archaeologist and now more and more people are moving into this field,' he says, with not a hint of resentment. 'There's still thousands of things to find. It would need me to live a thousand years to do it all.'

'It is a guessing game. You do have to use your imagination,' says Chris. 'We've a very interesting dig near Scales village, for instance, where the remains of possibly ten people have been discovered, seven of which are only around seven years old. We can't possibly begin to guess at the cause of death. Was it perhaps just a naturally high rate of infant mortality?'

Or was it something to do with the horrifying discovery Chris and his fellow archaeologists made when they examined the jawbones of the children more closely?

In each they found that the teeth were growing upside-down. The roots pointed upwards, exposed in the mouth. By some agonising genetic freak it seems that the second teeth of these hardy hunter-children were pointing into their gums.

Perhaps they starved to death, their bodies dumped in the mouth of a cave. Or worse, were they slaughtered to put them out of a misery even a modern-day dentist may have been appalled by?

As with so much of Chris Salisbury's work, the full picture will probably never be known.

way, and his skills couldn't count for long. Even when, as some say, he invented the first factory, he quickly followed it up with the first recession (long before the CBI). High above the treeline, in the mists of Pike O'Stickle, he'd fashioned the finest stone hand axes in Europe. In Germany and Gdansk, and all over Scotland and Wales, these grey, polished tools have been found and traced to the Langdale screes of Cumbria. For fifteen hundred years from 3,000 BC, a complex trading network had been built up to ferry the product of rain-battered mountain workshops to the tribal chieftains of less impoverished places.

But when metal came, Homo Northwestus was caught napping. He was so poor that he couldn't afford bronze, and, as the bottom fell out of the stone axe market, he drifted centuries behind the South (again) and the richer, eastern areas in the rain-shadow of this boggy patch – Yorkshire and Northumberland. As long ago as 1,200 BC, historians can detect a collapse in trading relations between northern and southern England. Homo Northwestus had nothing to sell, and could not brake his slide back into the darkness which Langdale's axes had all too briefly illuminated. No exotic goodies from Northern Europe reached these parts. There was no flow of ideas and currency. No white heat of pre-Christian technology. While Homo Northwestus sat with his head in the clouds, southern warriors were no doubt sharpening their hubcaps in the sunshine. This was not the Lancashire of myth. Why weren't we told?

▽ Imagine the scene before the drystone walls were built and before some hardy farmer decided to make his home out here upon these soggy moors . . . and you'll get an incling as to why upland Lancashire was so sparsely populated.

Now it is said that in Wigan, King Arthur had a fight, and that he once had a nap in Alderley Edge (a lot of people do); but in no reputable collection of Arthurian legends does he stalk up in these parts on any regular basis. Merlin never had a magic convention in Blackpool and, although the Round Table is doing fine things in Chorley, Excalibur there never was. Because when Merlin kissed in those mists of time, it was in Wessex and Wales and Strathclyde, not in the North-West. The age of Aquarius was at Glastonbury or Bath, and wherever King Arthur pulled the sword from the stone, it wasn't Manchester or Liverpool, or a theme park off the M6 near Charnock Richard. Here was an unpopulated bog, in the fog, on the edge of the world.

> ❛ Homo Northwestus lived in a bog, in the fog, at the edge of the world. ❜

Perhaps history will prove the Camelot theme park to be right. Perhaps King Arthur was indeed in Chorley, just as Lancashire took its name from Sir Lancelot, as some happy romantics still say.

It is believed, for instance, that his knights still haunt as ghosts at Rufford, near Southport, after dark. And in the writings of the ninth-century monk, Nennius, Arthur is clearly down for a series of battles on the banks of the river 'Dubglas'. Is this the River Douglas which flows through the Fylde flatlands into the tidal reaches of the Ribble?

Frank Walker certainly thinks so. Although he lives now at Old Hutton, near Kendal, he grew up near the Ribble and has become haunted more by the possibility that Arthur really was a Lancastrian than by the spirit of Sir Percival. His theory revolves around the Roman fort at Ribchester, where veteran Sarmatian cavalry, recruited by Marcus Aurelius in Hungary, may have stayed and married locally after the Empire collapsed. Was this the well-organised enclave which formed the basis of the Arthurian squads who battled, possibly against Irish intruders, on the banks of the *river 'Dubglas in regio Linnuis'*?

And was Linnuis what we now know as Lancashire? 'There are numerous rivers with the name Douglas,' argues Frank, 'but by 'Linnuis' Nennius may well have meant 'the region of the River Lune' which flows into Morecambe Bay at Lancaster which takes its name from the Lune.'

As yet – with research still underway – Frank remains cautious about claiming Ribchester as the true and authentic Camelot. Not that they'd move the theme park if it was proved, anyway. But he does have a theory about the Round Table which, in his view at least, lends a certain credence to his hypothesis.

'The Roman baths at Ribchester are very unusual in having a *laconium*, a circular, hot sauna-type of room about twenty feet in diameter. I wonder if the idea of Arthur's round table originated, not in a dining table, but in the relaxed after-duty atmosphere of a steam room?'

◁ At a point close to Heysham Church – here just visible through the foggy gloom of a January afternoon – and near to the nuclear power station St. Patrick is said to have landed after escaping from pirates . . . not that he stayed to enjoy the sights.

Always in the north it seemed that Homo Northwestus took a bashing. Even the main route north skirted his patch, crossing west at Scotch Corner to avoid his backward gaze. 'The most intensely isolated county,' it was said, and the timorous traders who travelled along Yorkshire's A1 ensured that it stayed so. There was to be virtually no pre-Roman Iron Age for Homo Northwestus. There was in the east. There were very few coins for Homo Northwestus. There were in the south and east. And even as the age of metal unfolded, there is little evidence that he discovered the Coniston copper only an arrow's flight from his Langdale axe factory. A bog, in the fog, at the edge of the world.

Not even the blandishments of the tourist industry can rewrite this absence of glory or triumph. In the English Heritage yearbook you can tot up the attractions and realise how deprived the North-West has been.

Latest scores . . .
Abbeys and ecclesiastical buildings: Lancashire 2, Yorkshire 10;
Castles and fortifications: Lancashire 0, Northumberland 10;
Prehistoric monuments: Lancashire 0, Wiltshire 11.

Apart from that rim round Morecambe Bay, the record of early man in the North-West is neither rich nor interesting. 'Nowhere can one experience a feeling of contact with the remote past, the indescribable feeling that the centuries of written history are as

▽ 'A feeling of contact with the remote past' . . . When the Castlerigg stone circle was built the Sphinx in Egypt may already have been four thousand years old.

nothing, that one feels in the shadow of a megalith in distant Cornwall.' So wrote historian Roy Millward in 1955, and little has emerged since to have shifted his perspective.

There are, however, some places where that 'indescribable feeling' can still penetrate the soul; blown off the Irish Sea, perhaps, on a dark, wet night by Heysham Head. Here is where St. Patrick washed up after a shipwreck, stopping only to draw breath before legging it back to his folks in Kilpatrick. Here is where the ancient rock-hewn graves lie, damp with saltwater, carved into the hard red cliff over a thousand years ago. Here the hot lime was mixed with broken seashells to bind the stones of St. Patrick's Chapel stoutly enough to bear nearly eleven centuries of westerly gales. But for all the mystery of places like this, it still doesn't amount to much.

△ The lids and the occupants have gone from these remarkable stone graves at Heysham. But who were they for?

And the purpose of this is not to demean or devalue Homo Northwestus. His later triumphs would overshadow and expunge almost all his dismal past. The purpose is, rather, to discover whether what Homo Northwestus is *now* – his character, his mood, his outlook – has more roots in a peat bog than a mill chimney. So much of what he thinks he was is an invention; an inherited set of fallacies; a Victorian myth saying that, because we were great then, it must always have been so.

In his prehistory, Homo Northwestus displayed a greater capacity for endurance of hardship than any other English species south of Hadrian's Wall. He had survived the indifference of climate and governments. Was he stubborn and hostile to change because of it?

How the Romans regarded this northern sub-species of bog people is unrecorded. One can only guess what they thought of the place. They had reached out from the banks of the Tiber, these civilising centurions, with their Latin and their swords, and at the edge of their empire was . . . Homo Northwestus – a pitiful thing who is not known to have put up much resistance. Only in North Wales, on Anglesey, were the tactical support groups of Julius Agricola given a run out with their spears. For these were policemen – keepers of the peace – whose presence in the North-West never civilised as it did in St. Albans or Cirencester in the South.

Not one Roman villa has been found between the North Cheshire Plain and Hadrian's Wall. Their buildings here were forts – cop shops – erected at key strategic points, where rivers met or roads crossed. No civilising, sophisticated Latins these. To the saturated wasteland that would become Wigan (*Coccium* in Roman times) were sent troops from Yugoslavia, Hungary and the Middle East; from France, Germany and Spain. The conscripts and the conquered who would be told: 'Keep the peace, we've got enough trouble in Scotland.' And so the legions would flow along the hilltop roads towards the wall: through Blackburn, Ribchester and Lancaster, to a place on the way they called . . . *medio bogdum*.

They must have dreaded being posted to the Hardknott Pass.

> 6 The Romans could have helped Homo Northwestus along – civilized him a bit – but it needed more than a few hundred reluctant soldiers to do it. 9

△   The Romans came to the North-West, saw it and conquered it, apparently without much difficulty. They didn't leave much of value behind, but some coins have been found, like these from Wigan.

▽   Can you imagine the reaction of the Latin conscripts when they were told that their next posting was to *medio bogdum* – a bleak, windswept frontier of Empire high up on the Hardknott Pass?

Even now, there's little enough decent chianti to be had nearby, and only on the rarest of summer days would the air have blown warm on their scarlet tunics. *Medio bogdum* was their name for this Cumbrian mountain fort, just as *Britannia Inferior* was how northern England would be labelled on a Roman map. *Britannia Inferior*? To the invading, occupying Italian forces, it was the fatter South of England which they named *Britannia Superior*. And although historians say the distinction was geographical, and not a measure of quality, one does wonder if Homo Northwestus, blissfully farming in his round huts, was at all offended.

Despite three centuries of Roman influence, Homo Northwestus was never to walk on a mosaic floor, never to share in those truer, nobler things born of an intelligent Empire. Soddus maximus there was here. No baths (hardly). No gardens on the vine. You can't brew frascati in Lancashire because the climate's just too awful.

It wasn't what the Romans did to Homo Northwestus that matters in this story. It's what they didn't do. All their money, all their best things, they passed to those collaborating Brits in the South. The villas with their underfloor steam heating were occupied by southerners whose sophistication, even before 'veni, vidi, vici', was in marked contrast to the lowly inhabitants of *Britannia Inferior*. Forget your southern sophistications: Homo Northwestus had already arrived breathless – into the Bronze Age. The Romans could have helped him along, shown him the ropes. But he needed more than a few reluctant conscripts for that.

The weather didn't help. Hard by Hardknott Pass are the wettest parts in all England and then, as now, Homo Northwestus took a rotten battering from the elements. When the black clouds blow in from the west they leave their worst here, reaching Yorkshire slim and fluffy. The Plain of Irlam doesn't look that different from the Vale of York, but its rainfall figures do. Yorkshire is drier, and when the skies open over the Wolds, the rain falls on much deeper, richer soil than our own.

The land around Blackpool and the Fylde wasn't always renowned for its tomatoes. It was mostly bog once; impenetrable, marshy swampland better suited to growing rice than corn. It was said that the area had more village idiots than anywhere else in England, owing to 'the dislike of people to marry outside the district,' and, because no-one came out, very few people went in. Not until the middle of the eighteenth century did the draining begin which transformed the primeval wastes into Lancashire's finest agricultural land. Imagine, then, this landscape before the Duke of Bridgewater reclaimed it with his ditches. The largest part of the Lancashire Plain was moss. Trafford Moss and Chat Moss to the west of Manchester; Rainford and Knowsley mosses; the Halsall moss; Martin Mere, and the twenty thousand acres of Pilling bog which, like God's grace, was said to be boundless. Lindow Man had even been found in a Cheshire bog, quite probably garrotted and lobbed there along with many others yet to be found.

This bog was part of Homo Northwestus's inheritance. It was no accident that new ideas laid only shallow roots in these remoter parts of his tribal homeland. When the Reformation came, it was to the Fylde

△ All the 18th- and 19th-century improvements and draining schemes removed such a lot of the good old-fashioned Lancashire bog that today relatively little remains. This lovely example is near Derwent Water in the Lakes.

that the recusant Catholics clung. This hostile, isolated land had bred a fear of change and now, faced with persecution, those same people found sanctuary in its remoteness. Never underestimate the hugely malign influence of Lancashire's geography on its people. Not until water became synonymous with power did it, or the climate, ever do Homo Northwestus any favours at all, and his glum pre-industrial nightmare really wasn't his fault.

Even as the ice melted it had robbed him of his finest ground. Eight thousand years before Christ the sea had risen, flooding the coastal plain between South Lakeland and North Wales. You stand on the prom at Morecambe and look out, and beneath the brine were some of our ancestors' finest hunting grounds, lost as the cold waters pushed back the North-West shoreline.

It wasn't his fault, either, that as the glaciers flowed they'd been kinder to the east than the west of the Pennines. Homo Northwestus didn't get the fertile, rolling hills packed with boulder clay that you'll find in what was (until Ted Heath) the East Riding. Often, those fine soils were left when the ice melted and the vast and powerfully wealthy monastic estates of Yorkshire – Rieuvaulx Abbey, Fountains Abbey – were a direct consequence of a freak which has become an inescapable fact. Homo Northwestus had

> **❛** It wasn't Homo Northwestus's fault. The climate and geography of the region was so isolated and inhospitable. **❜**

△ Huge swathes of natural woodland like this at Grizedale used to cover the useful bits of land between the coastal marshes and mosses to the west and the upland bogs and moors of the Pennines to the east.

pitched his tent on the wrong side of the country.

You can understand, too, that he might want to move out of his caves and sheds; clear away the trees that blocked his view; expand and move up onto the hillsides. But when Homo Northwestus cleared away the trees he made it worse. On the higher ground, peat bog took the place of elm and alder. The soil became infertile, hostile to refforestation, and the bleak moorland horizons so common across all today's North-West were created. There were woods once, and only the occasional petrified tree stump remains. Even now the Ordnance Survey marks the Forest of Rossendale where today the M66 slices towards Rawtenstall, past sewage treatment plants and DIY centres. There are no deer on the hoof here, no wild boar breaking wide-eyed out of cover. Even by Roman times, Homo Northwestus had rendered much of his upland patch untenable, and he was obliged to move lower, surrendering his old homesteads to the winds and the rain . . . and the peat.

f not the Romans, was it the Vikings who finally made Homo Northwestus what he is? They had come here mostly from Dublin, exiles of Norwegian and Danish origin chucked out of Ireland and re-settling in our thinly populated North-West. And when they came it was not, like Kirk Douglas or Tony Curtis in that old film, to carry away our women, our young men as slaves. No, these were peaceful people with horns on their cows, not on their helmets. Fishermen, not fighting men; and even this century in Flookburgh in Cumbria the locals still counted out their catch in Nordic numbers.

You can measure their presence in placenames. Hulme is Viking. So is Kirkham, and Lindale, and Myerscough which means 'boggy wood'. Sometimes the Irish roots of these Dublin Danes can be heard in Kirkby Ireleth ('the hillslope of the Irish') and Ireby Fell above Kirkby Lonsdale. For the best part of three centuries the Vikings' placid, pragmatic lifestyle filtered through and into the heart of Homo Northwestus. But it didn't shake, awake or inspire

▽ The Vikings came with horns on their cows not on their helmets . . . as fishermen not as fighting men. In Morecambe Bay their patterns of work live on.

him. 'These Danes,' wrote historian Frank Musgrove, 'were men of the soil with a grasp of detail and a total lack of imagination . . . wholly without vision or ideas'. Until recently, is this not how many outsiders, southerners, thought of twentieth-century Homo Northwestus? As the east grew ever richer, was Homo Northwestus growing ever more conservative, wary of outsiders and backward?

It's certainly true that when Sir Arthur Conan Doyle came to survey the brainpower of Homo Northwestus he found little evidence of intellectual advance since the Viking age. Sweeping broadly through Britain, he declared that Hampshire and Somerset had been our most 'distinguished' counties, Lancashire and Derbyshire the least. Using some inexplicable form of calculus, Conan Doyle deduced that the ratio of eminent men to Lancashire's total population was 1:74,000, suggesting that our heads were almost as empty as our pockets.

> **❛ The poorest county in England – ranked 38th out of 38 – before the coming of industry. ❜**

By almost any measure, it was true that before the nineteenth century Lancashire was the poorest county in England. In 1334 the tax returns on personal property made it the poorest out of all 38 counties assessed. 38th out of 38! Somerset was *thirty times* better off. Even by the early sixteenth century Lancashire is still bottom of the heap, and this poverty of the soil, this poverty of the spirit – how big a part of Homo Northwestus is that now?

So many things held him back, and so few people came to help. Even when they did he was wary and resentful, a suspicious species. Accidentally he'd turned the fells into peat bogs, and when the rain fell (as it did), he looked to himself. Unchanging, rural, Catholic Lancashire where, even until quite recently, coachloads would come to revere the parboiled head of priest Miles Gerard at St. Robert's Church, Catforth, on the Fylde: he'd been executed for his faith in 1590, his head impaled on a pike, the body quartered, his ears sliced off, and the grisly remains passed down to its resting-place on a faded church pillow.

Unchanging, rural, superstitious Lancashire where there lodged more Catholics than anywhere else, fighting the big new idea, clinging tightly, unto death, to the old ways. Homo Northwestus had had nowt and that's why, in Southport – and in Rochdale – he doesn't like the buses to change colour. For thirteen centuries, soddus maximus. *Medio bogdum. Britannia Inferior.* And, since nothing happened, we got rather fond of the *status quo*. Leave us be.

We're all right as we are.

And yet if he was such a race of small, insignificant, backward bog people, how did he, when his moment came, rise up to build monuments as great as the pyramids of Egypt? If for so long Homo Northwestus had been 38th out of 38, what magic lay dormant within him to get himself out of the bog?

The truth is that there was a hand outstretched to help and, reluctantly, Homo Northwestus grasped it.

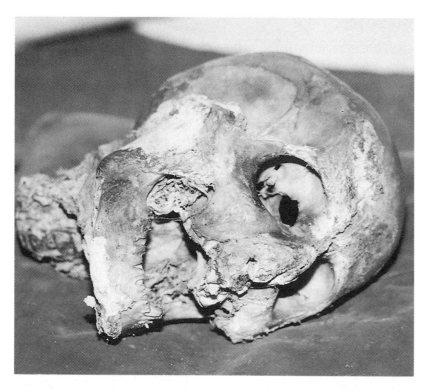

◁ The parboiled head of Blessed Miles Gerard. All the wonders of forensic science were employed to identify the remains (crucially, small pieces of lead shot were found behind one eye, and it is known that Miles had lost an eye in early life). The head is displayed in St. Robert's Church, Catforth, where the Rev. Fr. Hodson (below) shows it off proudly to visitors.

Chapter TWO

Out of the bog

T was cotton that transformed the fortunes of Homo Northwestus; the Industrial Revolution that rescued him from the bottom of the heap. For once he was going to be the right person in the right place at the right time. All the things that had for centuries held him back were now about to push him on.

Suddenly his habitat was on his side. He had lots of water and lots of coal laid down in ancient bog and now even the climate became a plus. Damp air was essential for spinning – if it was too dry the cotton would snap. In unfamiliar fine spells you had to re-create Lancashire's rain-soaked climate inside the mill with buckets of water tossed on the floor and open tanks of water steaming all day for humidity.

▽   Before the mills weavers worked at home in cottages like these at Ribchester.

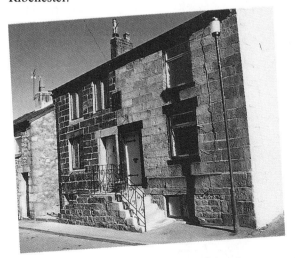

Perhaps more importantly, Homo North-westus for once even had the technology. As far back as the sixteenth century the poor terrain had forced farmers in the Pennine foothills to diversify to make ends meet. Their textile expertise stood them in good stead when cotton's moment came. Homo Northwestus had few boroughs and guilds and even this turned out to be an advantage, too, for it meant that vested interests did not stand in the way of new technology as was the case in plumper regions. Even Liverpool, for so long facing the wrong sea, was now the gateway to America.

From 38th out of 38 Lancashire shot up the county league table

◁ The weaving shed at Queen Street Mill in Burnley. The now silent (except for the tourists) face of Lancashire's great age.

of wealth. Towards the end of the nineteenth century Manchester was the richest city in the country outside London. Homo Northwestus was in demand – he had more money in his pocket than those in the agricultural South. In 1886 Lancashire textile millworkers could earn 15s 3d a week whilst their West Country counterparts could make only 10s 8d. Despite the overcrowding and feeble sanitation of the new urban sprawl Homo Northwestus had, in financial terms at least, never had it so good.

With the Industrial Revolution came a whole new world of work: the mills and the mass production; the industrial barracks of terraced streets and back-to-backs; the knockers-up in the morning; clocking-in; and even lip-reading in the new industrial din.

But Homo Northwestus couldn't manage on his own. Even with a local population explosion, outsiders were needed to build this

▷ Many of the early mills were spartan and utilitarian in design, but many later ones like this mill at Ancoats in Manchester were embellished with stone features, grand Italianate chimneys and huge expanses of windows.

new North-West and fuel this hungry revolution, and so offcomers poured in from all over England, Ireland, Scotland and Wales. Hands were needed to spin, to weave, to piece, to warp, to wind, to card, to grind, to oil, to sweep, to splice. Muscle was needed to navvy, to bricky, to slate, to roof.

And technical know-how was also needed: in St. Helens, Homo Northwestus needed French experts to help him make glass; in Cheshire, he needed the Germans to help him mine salt; whilst in Barrow-in-Furness, he needed the Cornish to help him extract the local iron ore.

Till now only a hardy handful had put down roots in the North-West. There were few memorials in stone to earlier versions of civilization – Liverpool would come to be our biggest city, but was only half a dozen streets when Exeter had a fourteenth-century cathedral. Now, brand new towns like Nelson (later to be described by Pevsner as having 'no past and no architectural shape') sprang up, and raw new mills and raw new ranks of terraced streets sprawled out from older centres, like boom-town Blackburn, whose population increased tenfold over the course of the century from 10,000 to 100,000.

> 6 Exeter had a medieval cathedral when Liverpool had only half a dozen streets and no parish church. 9

It was more like America here than any other part of the country. It wasn't just the new towns with their shallow industrial roots or the big opportunities for the daring entrepreneur, but the very volume of the immigrant mix swamping the aboriginal Northwestus as if he were a Red Indian in Chicago.

Historian John Smith of the University of Manchester's Department of Extra-mural Studies says the level of immigration meant that Lancashire was probably the most cosmopolitan area in England outside London. By 1851 almost a quarter of the population had been born outside the county – 10% were from Ireland, 3% from Scotland, and another 10% from other parts of England. But by then immigration had been taking place for nearly seventy years, and many Lancastrians were already the children of immigrant parents. Trying to find the genuine Lancashire article was beginning to be like trying to find the proverbial needle.

'Manchester and Liverpool became the great cosmopolitan towns of the region,' John Smith explains. 'By 1861, I calculate their populations were evenly divided between people born in Lancashire and incomers. As you move away from Manchester through the cotton towns, through Oldham and Rochdale and then north as far as Clitheroe, the proportion of foreign-born declines. So, if you're looking for the original, indigenous Lancastrians, you have to go north; beyond Manchester and Liverpool; beyond Warrington and Widnes; beyond Bolton and Oldham, and up into the country areas above Clitheroe.' John Smith is currently working on a history of Lancashire.

No-one could be a keener Lancastrian than Joan Hadwen.

▽ Ramsbottom. Its unspoilt Victorian streets make it the living essence of pure Lancashire. Or do they? The town as it is today was built by the Scots entrepreneurs, the Grants, and before they came there was nothing much here except wild garlic.

Originally from Accrington, she now lives in a bungalow in Morecambe and is in search of her Lancashire roots. She feels 'lucky to be more Lancashire than the Duke of Lancaster,' and is proud of her accent: 'I wouldn't have it knocked out of me. It's rich. It adds life. It's beautiful.' She remembers the Lancashire of the 'thirties: the clogs ringing on the flags; the shotgun weddings where brides 'got married with a big bouquet'; and the posters pasted up during the war declaring, 'England's bread hangs on Lancashire's thread'. She can trace her family back to 1591, to Sheephey Farm in deepest Lancashire, a stone's throw from the River Irwell above Ramsbottom. Her fourth great grandfather was John Kay, inventor of the flying shuttle. It seems an impeccable Lancashire pedigree but, even here, scratch and you'll find the ubiquitous outsider – this time Joan's great grandmother who came down from Paisley to

dilute the Lancashire line in the 1850s.

As old Lancashire disappeared under the tide of immigration, its culture and those of the new, often Celtic, immigrants began to fuse, and a new Lancashire began to evolve – a mongrel Lancashire – the Lancashire of the mills – which took definite shape with the nineteenth century and stayed that way until the Second World War. Ramsbottom is a part of it. It may sound as Lancashire as Stanley Holloway (who wasn't), but it's a mongrel mill town built out of Lancashire stone and a Scottish idea.

> ‘ Who is this new Homo Northwestus? Trying to find the genuine article – not some cardboard cut-out – is like trying to find a needle in a haystack. ’

It is said that, in 1783, the Grant family, farmers from Speyside newly ruined by flood and famine, paused at Top o'th'Hoof above the Irwell Valley overlooking the spot where Ramsbottom is today. Beneath them was 'a fair valley of trees and daffodils with a fine river meandering through lush meadows,' and, it is said, it reminded them of home. The Grants carried on south to Manchester in search of work and better fortune and, though unlucky there, managed to secure work from a fellow Scot, James Dinwoodie, in a calico printing works in Bury.

Over twenty years of hard Presbyterian graft later, the Grants came back to Ramsbottom, now consisting of a print works, two spinning mills and a scatter of cottages. This time they had money in their pockets. In 1806 they bought the Ramsbottom Printing Works from Sir Robert Peel, who was about to forsake Lancashire for the lordship of Drayton Manor in Staffordshire. Next, they bought the spinning mill in Nuttall village and, finally, in 1821, they commenced the building of their *tour de force*, the Square Mill, a nineteenth-century, state of the art 'manufactory'.

Fearful of industrial espionage, the Grants surrounded their new mill with a moat and there was only one entrance, over a drawbridge. Visitors who did manage to penetrate its security were impressed. It was described with enthusiasm in 1823 in *Chemical Essays*: 'The new works consist of four large edifices and as these are placed at right angles to each other they form a perfect square and enclose an area of more than an acre and a quarter. These buildings are all three storeys high and are lighted by nearly five hundred windows . . . In erecting this establishment the proprietors have studied neatness and elegance as well as usefulness; and

▷ St. Andrew's Church, Ramsbottom. Unlike Grants Tower, which collapsed in 1943, the family church has survived, its peculiar turreted spire visible for miles along the Rossendale Valley.

in the whole of their machinery they seem to have availed them-selves of every new invention.'

The Grants were not only model industrialists but were also known as model employers, to such an extent that Dickens used them as the inspiration for the benevolent Cheeryble brothers in *Nicholas Nickleby*. It is harder to know what their workforce and the descendants of their workforce made of these highly successful, entrepreneurial Scots. In 1828, some years after the death of their parents, the Grant brothers built a tower at Top o'th'Hoof in remembrance of them, but it is well decayed now, sliding into oblivion by the boarding kennels and the ITC transmitter. Their names do live on, however, down at St. Andrew's School where the school houses are called after the four Grant brothers. William, Charles, John and Daniel are still remembered by Ramsbottom's newest generation for their undeniable importance to the town.

The brothers are buried in St. Andrew's Church, whose dour exterior is fittingly more Presbyterian than Church of England. Built by William Grant and named after Scotland's patron saint, it began life in the non-conformist tradition, only to be anglicized by a second-generation Lancashire Scot, a Grant schooled at Eton. Only the family motto, *Craig Elachie* ('stand fast'), remains stubbornly in Gaelic over the door.

Inside it feels like the Grant mausoleum. There are nine Grant memorial tablets and not much space for anybody else. Hidden in the darkness at the back of the church is a memorial to an apparitor named Joseph Walker and, tucked away at the foot of the altar (which wasn't there when the church was first designed) is one to St. Andrew's first Anglican vicar. Otherwise the church commemorates the Grants exclusively. Though the tone is of unalleviated virtue, God is something of an also-ran.

There are no Grants left in Ramsbottom now. Several died childless and the nephew, John Grant Lawson, who inherited the lion's share of the family fortune, left Ramsbottom allegedly in a fit of pique after failing to be returned as the Member of Parliament for Bury. But the Grants could always find a job for a Scotsman and, though the family has faded out locally, the Scots are still here – and all over the North-West.

People have always been one of Scotland's major exports and, with so many of them educated, motivated and qualified at Scotland's older universities, they're used to taking up quarters here as doctors, dentists, engineers or, like the Grants, as entrepreneurs. They are still making the North-West a home from home; in Lancashire you could go out Scottish country dancing every night of the week and, in January, there are no end of Burns dinners. The North-West Scots even have their own chieftain. Just now it is Burton McLeod who came down to Manchester in 1960 and started his own office cleaning business. He thinks the Scots are accomplished nomads; adaptable, useful, never ending up in the ghetto trap. Exile suits the Scots, he thinks, but they sense a particularly kindred spirit in the North-West. Maybe, he hazards, it's a common sense of grievance and resentment at southern domination.

The high point of Burton's calendar is the day when Balmoral comes to Blackpool – when the Lancashire and Cheshire Federa-

△ Bill Shankly, Kenny Dalglish . . . people have always been one of Scotland's major exports.

tion of 56 Scottish Societies holds its annual Highland Games in the curiously inappropriate flatlands of Stanley Park. Here you'll find kilts to the right of you and kilts to the left of you and, everywhere, filling your ears, the skirl of the pipes. Behind the arena you'll find huddled knots of pipers tuning up; solo drummers rehearsing their staccato phrases; and performers by their open car boots, gingerly pulling on their tartan underwear. Inside the arena they'll be doing the Fosbury Flop in kilts, performing Highland dances with pumped precision and tossing the caber (though not with any visible success). And everywhere there will be the most intense scrutiny, for the Games are a serious business. Perhaps fiercest of all are the pipe band judges, pacing round the bands in dour circles, clipboard clutched to ear against distraction. The day ends with a march past of the massed pipe bands, with Burton taking the salute alongside the Mayor of Blackpool.

But, though the accent is on all things Scottish, the voices you overhear are more likely to be Lancashire and Scouse than Glasgow and Morningside. Jimmy Conway is the bass drummer of St. George's Pipe Band, Chorley, which plays in the Macbeth tartan and practises twice a week every week. Jimmy came down in 1966 – 'the year England won the World Cup' – but he still feels 100% Scots, and his Glasgow accent hasn't faded one iota. 'If I wasn't a Scotsman,' he says, 'I'd want to be one.' But he is an exception in the band; only one of them is Scottish, one is Irish, the others are from Chorley. Though Jimmy used not to think a Lancashire man could play the pipes, he's been forced to change his mind: 'There are times when they make the hairs on the back of my neck stand on end'.

It's hard to believe that at the beginning of the Industrial Revolution Homo Northwestus showed such enthusiasm for the pipes. Bypassed and backwatered for centuries, he had been unused to strangers and was really rather shy. At the very least, incomers could be culture-shocked by this brave new world. John Smith told us what it must have been like to arrive in Lancashire as the industrial culture began to take root. 'It's difficult to realize that people from Buckinghamshire, for example, were just as foreign as people from Scotland or Ireland. A Dr. Kay, who was writing about the 1830s, said that newcomers here from Buckinghamshire were appalled by their new neighbours, by their apparent rudeness, their briskness of manner, their punctuality, their restless energy. Everything about them was foreign – and they didn't like the incomers.'

> 6 It may sound heretical, but the idea that Lancashire was warm-hearted and friendly and glad-handing to newcomers was just not true. 9

Though Homo Northwestus needed strangers, he wasn't always kind to them. It may sound heretical, but the idea that Lancashire was warmhearted and friendly and glad-handing to newcomers was just not true. Mill owners welcomed outsiders because they were cheap labour, but working people saw them as a threat.

The Irish were particularly unpopular. They could afford to take lower wages than the Lancashire workers and still be far better off than they had been before. In Ireland an ordinary labourer might earn about a shilling a day; on the mainland he could make twelve shillings a week. In any case, the Irish frequently had little intention of staying longer than a few months in the North-West – just long enough to earn the passage money to America.

Employers used the Irish quite cynically as a tool to keep wages down. The Rev. Campbell of Liverpool outlined the strategy in a report of 1854: 'In the present state of the labour market,' he reported, 'English labour would be almost unpurchaseable if it were not for the competition of Irish labour. The English labourers have unfortunately been taught their rights till they have almost forgotten their duties . . . and in that case we are very frequently able to put on the screw of Irish competition.'

Sometimes racial hostility would erupt into violence. In 1839, 250 English and three hundred Irish labourers engaged in a three-day battle on the line of the Chester and Birkenhead Railway. A year earlier, English weavers and Irish navvies had tangled on the North Union Railway near Preston. In Manchester it had become common practice to keep Irish weavers and English weavers apart.

> ❛ The Irish, in particular, were unpopular because they would take low wages and because their destitute were a burden to the ratepayers. ❜

▽ In total it has been reckoned that about 8 million people have emigrated via Liverpool.

Famine brought the Irish to Lancashire by the hundred thousand. Between 1847 and 1853 over a million and a half landed in Liverpool, crossing the Irish Sea on steamers where the competition for passengers was so stiff there was even a price war. Frank Neal of Salford University has pointed out that the port had steamer connections with Cork, Waterford, Wexford, Port Rush, Londonderry, Sligo, Belfast, Dublin, Drogheda, Dundalk and Newry. 'By 1847,' Neal writes, 'Liverpool was like a town under siege.'

More than half the Irish emigrants were *en route* to the new worlds of Australia and America, but the remainder – the poorest of the poor – stayed on, absorbed into Liverpool with its overcrowded courts and cellars and its growing tradition of casual, unskilled labour. It was alleged that Irish landlords and even the Irish authorities were paying the passage of the immigrants in order to get them off their hands. The resentment of the Liverpool ratepayers was unbounded – the Famine cost them in the order of £70,000.

By 1851 the Irish-born population of Liverpool was 83,813, almost a quarter of the whole city. If, in addition to this figure, you were to take into account the generations of children in Liverpool already born to Irish parents, it is debateable, as Frank Neal comments, whether Liverpool was English at all. As well as such huge concentrations in Liverpool, many of the Irish had, by the 1840s, settled in Manchester, Stockport, St. Helens, Wigan and Preston. Lancashire was the most Irish county in England.

The Irish were not just unpopular because their workers would take low wages and because their destitute were a burden on the taxpayer. They were unpopular because they were different. The stories of the Paddy with the pig, the croft in the backyard, were true and their tradition of rural living fitted in very badly with the new urban world. The Irish brought with them their own religion, their own culture, their own drinking habits and in some members of Homo Northwestus they elicited a frightening racial hatred. The *Liverpool Herald*, in 1855, called them the 'Curse of Liverpool': 'It is remarkable and no less remarkable than true, that the lower order of Irish papists are the filthiest beings in the habitable globe, they abound in dirt and vermin and have no care for anything but self gratification . . . Look at our police reports, three fourths of the crime perpetrated in this large town is by Irish papists. They are the very dregs of society, steeped to the very lips in all manner of vice, from murder to pocket picking and yet the citizens of Liverpool are taxed to maintain the band of ruffians and their families in time of national distress'.

Sectarian riots resulted. In 1852 the Catholic sunday school procession in Stockport ended in a three-day religious feud – the first of many anti-Irish riots which were to rock the cotton towns for the next twenty years. It was to take a generation before most sectarian conflicts finally flickered out, though in Liverpool the Irish remained an issue for a good while longer; in 1918 Sinn Fein even won the Exchange seat. And it was to Liverpool too, of course, that the Irish left a less contentious inheritance. Before the 1840s Liverpudlians had spoken with a Lancashire accent; afterwards, they spoke in Scouse.

Now it seems that Manchester has a more vibrant Irish community than Liverpool. There are over twenty Irish county associations to remind exiles of their Cavans, Kilkennys or Clares, and last year saw the Fourth Manchester International Set Dance Festival at the Forum in Wythenshawe. And in Cheetham Hill you'll find not just another Irish social club where you can sip a congenial pint of Guinness, but the Irish World Heritage Centre, whose aim is no less than to make people aware of the contribution of the Irish worldwide. You can eat Irish food here, dance Irish dance and learn the Irish language. The Centre was begun in 1982 and built with voluntary Irish labour – its main bar is built out of

▷ There's more work around Manchester now, where the Irish community is dedicated to the celebration of its culture. Today it seems to be Manchester, more than Liverpool, where the true Irish heartbeat can be measured.

real timber to look like a traditional Irish cottage, with a jackdaw on the thatch and an Aer Lingus airliner hovering overhead. Michael Ford, the Centre's guiding light, has ambitious plans for its development: Phase Two will have a traditional pub, an exhibition, a library and a cinema; and Phase Three will have an athletics track, craft workshops and, finally, a hotel.

Michael is not the only one to be busy building Ireland here in the North-West. Paddy Johnson came over from County Offaly in 1963 to look for work here, as generations of his compatriots had done before him. Now he is a prosperous regional sales manger, married to a wife from County Donegal and the father of two boys and two girls. But Paddy says he is no Homo Northwestus – he is Irish through and through: 'If I had the opportunity to go back and get a decent job and keep the standard of living that I've got here I'd go back tomorrow as well as would my wife. In fact she'd go back tomorrow one way or the other . . . It'll always be home to us'.

The Irish are so well organized now in the North-West that they even have their own Gaelic football league, and Paddy is a committed supporter and referee of the game. He'll supervise matches such as that between Oisin in the blue hoops and St. Brendan's in maroon and, though the setting may be the draughty playing fields of Hough End in South Manchester, there is always something exotic in the air. It's not just the team names but the naming of names on the touchlines, with one coach shouting, 'Come on, John Finnegan,' and another, 'You've plenty of time Declan Murphy'.

But Gaelic football can't survive here on the Irish-born alone. It relies on second and third generation Irish to keep it flourishing. There are some who play with no Irish connections at all; a coloured boy plays for St. Lawrence's in Manchester, and a Chinaman turns out for one of the Liverpool teams. Even an Englishman could play. Even Ray Gosling . . . ?

'And could an Englishman play?', asked Ray.

'Englishmen, certainly', replied Paddy.

'But it's Irish.'

'It's an Irish game.'

'If I played often enough I might become an Irishman.'

'Well, we're willing to give you a try. We welcome everybody.'

The North-West is still a very cosmopolitan place and today our entrepreneurs are just as likely to be immigrants as were the Grant brothers or Friedrich Engels over a hundred years ago. Joe Bloggs, said to have put Manchester on the fashion map, is the brainchild of Shami Ahmed, his family being from Delhi via Karachi. Salford Van Hire is the creation of Raffaello Bacci from Lucca in Tuscany. It's not that other places didn't get immigrants too, but more of them came to the North-West when the North-West was next to nothing, and they settled by almost every mill in every valley. The immigrant *became* Homo Northwestus, though many never lost a part of themselves, a corner of them always loyal to their ancestors, like the Irish in New York.

Sometimes the process of becoming absorbed by the tribe seemed slow; Paddy Johnson's children, for example, feel every bit as Irish as he does. Not only do they take part in Irish games, but Paddy talks of how they choose to go 'home' for their holidays – and he isn't talking about South Manchester. Though born and bred here, he says they would settle in Erin's green valleys tomorrow.

For some of our newer immigrants there is no such reluctance to adopt a new identity; they are naturalized Northwesti. In the 1960s the Asians came to Lancashire's now-dying cotton towns to take up employment at lower pay for longer hours, just as the Irish had done over a century before. Sardar Khan Sharif is one of them. Now in his mid-thirties, tall and statuesque, dignified in long grey tunic and white skull cap, he seems more mullah than business-man. He has the *gravitas* of a man twice his age. His father came over from Pakistan in 1960 to work in the textile mills of Black-burn. He wasn't technically qualified, but he didn't need to be, for work in the mills was unskilled. His wife and four sons, of whom Sardar is the eldest, joined him after five years.

Sardar began work in 1970, at first in the mills and then, after an injury, collecting cardboard boxes from all over Lancashire to sell to the paper mills for £5 a day. There was no let-up; the younger members of the family were still being educated and the family needed the money. In 1979, with the mills in terminal decline, the Sharifs bought their first shop, 81 Johnstone Street. They've kept the doors open now for thirteen years, from 7.00 in the morning till 9.30 at night. They soon put the Co-op next door out of business: 'They relied on staff and policies; we relied on family, hard work, long hours, and better prices – we could set our own profit margins'.

It was the beginning of an empire. Sardar took us on to the street and pointed out the shops: 'That's ours,' he said of the chemist's, 'and that,' of the post office, 'and that,' of the hardware shop. Each

business is run by a member of the family.

Sardar's brother qualified in pharmacy at Leicester University and afterwards wanted to work in London, but Sardar persuaded him to come home. 'I said to him, we have spent most of our lifetime here. From teenage up to now. And our father has worked here – worked hard. You've been educated here. We know the people. We have more chances here than in the South. So . . . after very hard discussions, he agreed to stay.'

Sardar's third brother is the postmaster and the fourth, Ifthik Har (though the locals affectionately call him Harry) works in the grocer's. The whole family lives together. Though Islamically teetotal, their dynastic home, next to the shop, is the Pineapple, originally a sizeable pub and still resplendent with crimson bench seats and flock wallpaper. They are an extended family: the

△ Sardar Khan Sharif . . . in his mid-thirties, tall and statuesque, dignified in a long, grey tunic and white skull cap. 'I trusted here. I believed in it. I have sacrificed going home. So I want to stay here . . . I believe I can call myself a British Muslim living in the North.'

patriarchal Mr and Mrs Sharif live here, calm, polite and retiring, and the house is busy with the comings and goings of many children. Though the Sharif empire is undoubtedly a prosperous one – Sardar reckons they serve between five and six hundred customers a day – there is little sign of conspicuous consumption. Presumably the family's assets are all invested in their future.

On the surface this may seem a brand new Lancashire, but in many ways it is an older Lancashire underneath – living on the Coronation Street principles. Sardar has a theory: 'These terraced houses are very helpful because you are living next door to each other. If you're in London, you have big houses. You don't meet people for five or ten years. But here you meet daily. Whenever you go out you say, "good morning," or "good afternoon," or "good evening". Saying hello and meeting people gives us more of a chance to understand each other'.

And it certainly sounds like Lancashire. Leading Yorkshire phoneticist Stanley Ellis says that immigrant children frequently have much stronger local accents than indigenous children. He thinks it's because their parents don't try to make them speak 'properly' when they get home from school. Sardar's children certainly speak pure Blackburn and Sardar himself, though he speaks still with an Asian accent, calls out, 'What's to do?' in irreproachable Lancashire when he hears one of the children crying.

> 6 Though he still speaks with an Asian accent he calls out "What's to do?" in pure Lancashire when one of his children is crying. 9

The Sharifs are also a religious family. Their children attend the mosque every evening at 7 o'clock to read the Koran and to take religious instruction in Punjabi and English. Sardar has been on pilgrimage and several members of his family were newly returned from Mecca, but, though inspired by a strong sense of culture, Sardar sees no problem of identity. The North-West is home – his children are good British Muslims. He is Homo Northwestus.

Ray asked, 'You won't go back to Pakistan, to live, to settle?'

'Well it's a very hard question. I won't be able to. All the achievement, all the hard work and all the struggle of my life are here. I trusted here. I believed in it. I have sacrificed going back home. So I want to stay here. I want to enjoy my family treasure, you see – what we have built up. I want to see people respect my children and my family . . . so I believe I can call myself a British

Muslim living in the North.'

Sardar's dynasty has deliberately put down its roots. It's here to stay. But not all incomers have had such clear intentions. Many Irish and Scots seem to be here because their ancestors got left behind when the boat sailed without them. Lord Derby (see Chapter 5) told us how would-be emigrants to Canada or America 'used to get as far as Liverpool, have a good night out, miss the boat and then settle down in Liverpool'.

Many of our Jews, too, were accidental arrivals. Two million of them were on the road in the 1880s, refugees escaping mass persecution in Russia and heading for the Home of the Free. They left Eastern Europe for the North Sea ports of London, Hull and Newcastle. Some thought they were on a non-stop passage from Danzig to the USA and were a bit surprised to find Hull was not America. But most were heading for Liverpool – the front door to New York.

Many paused in Manchester, meaning only to stay long enough to earn the £10 it would cost to pay for their passage to the USA, but, says Werner Mayer, Chairman of the Trustees of the Manchester Jewish Museum, 'they got fed up, they'd had enough, they said, "We'll go next year," and they're still here'.

The new immigrants were not posh, they were penniless. They spoke their own language, they dressed conspicuously, they made raincoats – 'in Manchester, where else,' comments Werner. They

◁ Werner Mayer giving what the photographer Ian Beesley described as the most entertaining talk he'd heard, to a group of schoolchildren in Manchester.

invented the rag trade. They lived in the Redbank and Strangeways areas of Manchester and the established Jews were sorry for them – but hoped they wouldn't marry their daughters. Even the poor Jews, though, scaled the social ladder. It took a couple of generations, but the 'My son, the doctor,' Jewish syndrome came to pass here as elsewhere.

Werner himself arrived more by accident than design. He came to Manchester via Dachau and has never forgotten how lucky he is to be alive. He was born in a small provincial town, Landau, near Heidelberg, where there had been a Jewish community since the twelfth century. When anti-semitism became official state policy in 1933 the family stayed on, thinking it couldn't last forever. In any case they had nowhere else to go. By 1938, they were in Dachau, though it was not yet an extermination camp.

Werner's mother, in despair, wrote to an old acquaintance who had left Landau for Manchester in 1933, and the seventeen year old Werner was fixed up with a student visa. It was supposed to be a temporary move. He was merely to bide his time in England whilst waiting for an American visa. In the meantime Werner took a job in a bakery and was shortly afterward interned as an enemy alien until his US visa came through. His parents stayed on in Germany 'with the other six million'.

Werner's visa came through during the war – but he never used it. He met his late wife, Lena Alvarez, was engaged and married in the Spanish and Portuguese synagogue, where the Museum is now. In 1947 they had the chance to go to Israel, but they missed it: 'There comes a time when it's too late . . . Time takes its toll'.

Werner and Lena had no children, but Werner insists that if he had, 'they would have been brought up in a Jewish household, entered for a Jewish education and, as they grew up, introduced to the idea of visiting Israel maybe with the hope that they would find their destiny in that country'. But Werner won't leave now. He'll live the rest of his life in Manchester and he will be buried here, though it won't be entirely in North-West soil: 'We have our own pattern of dealing with that last journey . . . we spread some *terra santa*, some soil from the land of Israel, upon the deceased. So when I do find my last resting place it will be in a peculiar blend of Manchester and Israel'.

Werner loves Lancashire: he finds it a brilliant amalgam of people from all over the world; he loves North Manchester, where he has settled; he loves the hills. But he says he won't, if you visit

Manni Passerini will cut your hair in Mincing Lane, Blackburn. Go into his shop and there he is, looking composed and exotic in his black silk shirt and the longest moustache north of Sicily. That's where he came from in 1963, 'for the future, for the better life,' although he didn't step outside of his brother's house for six months, so bitterly did he feel the cold.

He'll welcome you – and ask how you want it – in Italian Blackburnese, but lapse easily, comfortably, into Italian with his sons Luigi, Michael, Giuseppe, each with Blackburn on their birth certificates but Palermo in their hearts. They'll speak Italian at home, too, drinking Casa Passerini wine with a 'salute' not a 'cheers'. And though they support Juventus and would rather eat pasta than fish and chips, they're here to stay now. 'I spent the best of my life in Blackburn, says Manni. 'Italian I am by birth, but England gave me everything.'

him, offer you black pudding and tripe. 'There is no clear cut fence between my identities – I'm as complex as the next fellow.' Whilst part of him calls Lancashire home, there is still a homesickness for Jerusalem.

As Werner says, Homo Northwestus is a complex kind of a fellow – intractably a mongrel. But walk around Manchester's Southern Cemetery – immense and sprawling – and you can see how often the old roots push back through. Together, at the end, are the Armenians, the Jamaicans, the Chinese, the Jews; each grouped in the lines of their own tribal plot. Buried in the end in his old ethnic cages Homo Northwestus can often, in his short spell here, seem a mite provisional. It is as if he is only here in body – quite likely to be pushing his shopping around Sainsbury's while his mind is in Majorca or Mayo.

But even mongrels can, in time, evolve a distinctive voice, distinctive values and trademarks – even a distinctive diet – and in corners of the North-West you can still be sure you're really nowhere else.

Chapter THREE

A mon like thee

'Dad of us all dwells theer up i't'welkin. What they caw thee's trett reyt holy.

May thi thowts reach as far as eawr intek, an' let's hev things done i't'world deawn 'ere t'same rooad as tha has done i'thy pleck up theer.

Afoore t'day's eawt, let's aw of us hev summat t'eyt, an let us off fer what we've done wrong like, same way as we mun let off them as has done amiss by us . . .'

The Lord's Prayer, adapted in Lancashire dialect by Harvey Kershaw

◁ Two images of declining industrial Lancashire. The massive bulk of the tobacco warehouse at Stanley Dock, Liverpool, waits, forlorn, for a decision about its fate as conservationists and developers argue over its architectural merits and design limitations. No such doubt lingers over the fate of Bickershaw Colliery (below), which will shortly cease mining in an area that used to bristle with pithead winding gear.

There are over seven million in the tribe Homo Northwestus, but how many of those recite the Lord's Prayer in Lancashire dialect on any regular basis? How many eat tripe? How many in the modern North-West region wear clogs? How many of your friends and neighbours race whippets? Some will; it hasn't all gone. And yet, to so much of the world, this is what Homo Northwestus is. How many George Formby CDs do they sell each day in W. H. Smith's? How many union shirts (100% pure wool) do they stock in Dunn's? The mills have mostly gone now, and our cotton tea towels will probably be made overseas; yet these crass images of mucky industrial Lancashire still endure. Why?

To members of the wider world who never stray north of Hatfield, there may only be Lowry prints and George Formby films to support their view. Small wonder that for these southern image-makers Homo Northwestus really *is* a species of little matchstalk men, his clogs clattering, clip-clopping and sparking down the cobbles from the mill, his face fixed in a gormless, cheery, imbecilic smile.

And always on that face, it seems, are the features of George; as if, when that man opened his mouth, all of Homo Northwestus was lumped together – Cheshire, too – in one, common, toothy grin. An image so strong, so popular and so exportable that in foreign parts the North-West is time-warped; its people forever frozen silhouettes on a painting by a Salford artist. But if the flat cap fitted then, surely it doesn't fit now, when so few of us even wear them any more. Colin Crompton's dead. L. S. Lowry's dead. And yet this is the image Homo Northwestus has – just as Paris has the can-can, and London the beefeater or pearly queen. It's a corporate logo, an inherited crest – two black puddings resting on a moist bed of mushy peas – which has stuck fast and is showing itself to be very durable indeed.

The North-West has changed and moved on, and even when those industrial landscapes *were* a true picture they represented only a very small part of the whole. When Lowry picked up his brush he was painting Salford and Oldham, not the Trough of Bowland, or Silverdale. The way of life he portrayed could be found only in certain confined places. Although the belt of north-east Lancashire mill towns bulged alarmingly with people, there were still other folk – from the dairy farmers of Cheshire to the fishermen of Flookburgh – to embrace as Homo Northwestus.

> 6 The flat-cap image still peddled by southern image-makers was as unrepresentative then as it is now. 9

In other words, this flat cap image of our species was as unrepresentative then as it is now. It was only part of what we have already demonstrated was a rich mix of race and creed, language and culture. Nevertheless, the image prevailed; and it did spring truly from a way of life that was unique to Homo Northwestus.

Its heartland spread down from the Pennines through Oldham and Rochdale, taking in Bury, Bolton, Burnley and Blackburn on a sprawling, grey-slate smear which pulled up at Wigan and Warrington just short of the Mersey shoreline. Within this proud red-brick jungle, people helped and protected each other, and communities drew loyally tight to themselves. But now it's fading and, as traditional industries wither, what qualities of old Homo Northwestus might we lose and regret in this new North-West? As mill towns re-invent themselves as shopping arcades, what price those prized Lancashire virtues of open-doored neighbourliness and straight-talking simplicity? What remains of those things that other people expect Homo Northwestus to be?

To find out what is left, head north out of Manchester up the M66 towards the Rossendale Valley. Don't stop in Ramsbottom (which has the look, but not the authentic feel, of disappearing Lancashire), but carry on up towards Bacup, which has yet to suffer the sandblasting embrace of city suburbia. It's along remoter valleys like this, with its Waterfoot and Stacksteads, that older traces still survive. The occasional chimney still smokes, the slate roofs stack up against peaty skies and, wherever travelling times still thwart incomers and outsiders, an older, less diluted, less mobile population has clung on. People like Emma Edge who, although as old as the century, still shines sweetly in the terraced house she has lived in since she 'were wed' in 1925.

In Emma's house a cup of tea isn't offered out of good form – it's part of an obligatory social ritual which lays down that no serious chat can take place without one. That carefully warmed pot, with its lacquer of tannin, is more than a brew – it's a demonstration of communal warmth; just as Emma's distinction between religious people and Christians maps out the unique ethos of threatened Lancashire.

△ Emma Edge: the true spirit of old, unfashionable industrial Lancashire.

'To me there's a lot of difference to being a Christian and being religious,' says Emma. 'Being religious, I think, it's like Sunday and they put it away at Monday. If you are a Christian you will live with it every day.'

Emma grew up on a farm, but spent most of her working life at Broad Clough Mill weaving 40-inch wide rolls of cotton, while her husband shod the hooves of Bacup's milk float horses. Starting at six in the morning, she'd work for two hours before breakfast, then through till 5.30 with an hour's break for snap. But in Emma today there is no winsome nostalgia for this bygone era with its punitive conditions of labour, its cold bedrooms and statutory holidays in Morecambe or in friendship homes at Colwyn Bay. 'It's better now for a lot of things,' she reckons. 'We had no electric lights, nor gas. We had oil lamps and a coal fire and all the cooking were done in the fire oven or on the fire . . . When we used to be at home we had nowt that was labour saving, just a great big set pan in t'corner we had to boil clothes in. Do you want sugar in your tea?' And with that, Emma is off, worrying a set of unchipped cups out of her corner cupboard for another brew, while informing Ray Gosling that, although he might persist in his 'cheeky' line of questioning, she won't necessarily provide him with all the answers.

'What makes Lancashire special, do you think?', asks Ray.

'Do you know? I don't know. I wouldn't. I will tell truth, I think Old England's best country there is and I wouldn't like to live anywhere else. Would you?'

'Sometimes.'

'Eee. I wouldn't and I've never been abroad . . . although it's true people's not as friendly as in olden times. When I first come here in this street there were a lot of friendliness but it's not so good now although 'er next door is very nice, you know. I get on well with 'er. They don't go into one another's houses like they used to, do they? I remember I was in this street and there were a woman and they went on holiday and they left both back and front door open. And do you know there weren't a thing missing when they came back. Not a thing.'

She wouldn't leave her doors open herself. Not now. And in Bacup, just like everywhere else, red and yellow alarm boxes have spread like contagious spots on the walls of homes and shops. For people who remember a different way, there's a sadness in this which outweighs the material advantages which the twentieth century has latterly won for its working people. Hospitality was a code which Homo Northwestus celebrated and, in the pub vault of his favourite alehouse, songs would be invented by nameless taproom composers.

> *There's an owd man lives down our street in a cozy cottage house*
> *and on a Sunday morning if it's fine*
> *I often goes to sit wi' him to 'ave a smoke or chat*
> *because he is a dear owd friend of mine.*
> *And when it's getting dinnertime and dinner's ready then*
> *and I thinks it must be time for me to go.*
> *Well he goes and hangs mi 'at up just behind the owd front door*
> *and then to my surprise I 'ear 'im say . . .*
> *Eee Ah'm allus glad fo't'see a mon like thee.*

> ❛ When we used to be at home we had nowt that was labour saving, just a great big pan set in t'corner we had to boil clothes in. ❜

Tha's as welcum lad as welcum as can be.
Fotch thi chair reet up to t'table,
Stop as long as thou are't able,
For Ah'm allus glad fo't'see a mon like thee.

How many eat tripe? Emma Edge does. She'll take it warm with onions or cold with a splash of salt and vinegar. Cow-heels she'll boil up with shin beef to make a nice potted meat, but pigs' trotters are not to her taste and black puddings only cross her lips, as she puts it, 'about once every twelve-month'. These foods have become more than just things that a very few of us regularly eat. In France they'll serve tripe minced into sausages as a delicacy, but to Homo Northwestus it's much more than that. It's a badge; a reminder that Lancashire was once so poor, a place where poverty-wrecked families scraped to survive, not on the best cuts, but on offal. Cows' udders and sheeps' heads were the food then because they were cheap and 'our childer' were starving. Chicken nuggets would probably be cheaper now. So do these foods survive because it's a choice that the older Homo Northwestus makes – as if not to make that choice would be to let go of something culturally precious?

> 6 "I'd hate to see the tripe business end", he says looking proudly into a vat of boiling cows' feet. 9

And however cosmopolitan the species has become – pizza in Preston, rogan josh in Runcorn – there is still enough life left in tripe for the likes of Les Hayhurst to keep ticking over. It's nearly twenty years since he struck out in tripe, starting as a driver before running and eventually owning his own business behind Padiham market. 'I'd hate to see it end,' he says, looking proudly into a vat of boiling cows' feet. 'I eat it a lot and what I say is you're in no danger of salmonella from this lot. It's boiled for so long that it's very safe.'

And so it is; but only the strongest of human stomachs should do anything more than *eat* the linings of cows' stomachs: the gurgling cauldrons of Les's tripe factory will eventually deliver tender, creamy frills to dress butchers' windows from Wigan to Walkden, but the process that creates them is definitely not for the squeamish. Fresh from the slaughterhouse, the stomachs are soaked, scraped and boiled twenty-five at a time before a degreasing machine removes the fat which, in Les's words, is 'very, very unpopular these days'.

Homo Northwestus likes his tripe colourless. Not like in Italy, where they take it as it comes, but a milky, platinum blonde colour which follows an overnight soak in a bathful of diluted hydrogen peroxide. 'Actually you've more taste with it before you bleach it,' points out Les, who's 65 and a true connoisseur. 'But we wouldn't sell it if we didn't take the colour out. We used to sell some to an Italian restaurant, but he wouldn't have it bleached because that's not the way in Italy. Here I suppose we just started whitening it a long time ago and it's what people have got used to.'

And, because in the mists of history Homo Northwestus had nothing, nothing is wasted. The fat from the tripe is sold to the tallowman, and the oil skimmed off the boiling cow heels is used for softening harnesses, or as a local remedy for the symptoms of rheumatism. It's a simple life, this Lancashire life, and although now just an echo of the past, there is still enough to keep Les in bustling business, with few complaints about trade. In this low-cholesterol age he can still point to his dad, who loved his tripe and his cows' udders, who inhaled his twist tobacco, and who cherished life until he was 85 years young.

Butcher, butcher, give us a sheep's head.
I can't afford to buy fresh meat.
But, butcher, please don't pull its eyes out.
It's got fo't see us all through next week.

Songs and rhymes like these are another echo of those Lancashire scenes which have proved so internationally strong. Homo Northwestus, with his industrial revolution, had invented a new way of life and devised a culture with which to celebrate it. Unsophisticated street songs, a matchstalk man, an ode to a boy, a lion and a zoo. To meet the needs of the mills, streets had sprung up where people lived and were united by hard work and shared poverty; a life of tripe until July, when they'd sing and laugh their way to Blackpool for Wakes holiday, while the

Tripe king Les Hayhurst of Padiham doesn't just sell tripe, he swears by it. 'When my tummy's a bit upset it's better than a bottle of medicine,' he says, pointing as proof to a British Medical Association booklet published in the 1940s. *All about Tripe* spares no compliment in its flattery of these flaccid flaps of cow. Dozens of recipes are set out, some with the principal aim of camouflaging the central ingredient from those too queasy to eat it in its natural state. Here, as an example, is one suggested meal:

Tripe Hotpot (serves 4)

1lb pre-cooked tripe
1lb onions
2lb potatoes
Stock
1 tablespoon beef dripping
1oz flour
3 tomatoes
salt and pepper

Wipe the tripe, cut it up and dip the pieces in seasoned flour. Peel and slice the onions and potatoes, and tomatoes. Now fill a greased casserole dish with alternate layers of tripe and vegetables, seasoning each layer as you go. The bottom and top layer should be potato. Pour stock halfway up the layered ingredients and dot the dripping on the top. Cover with a lid and cook for ninety minutes at gas mark 5/ 375°C. Take the lid off for the final hour in order to brown the top. Serve and enjoy.

△ Les Hayhurst doesn't just sell tripe; he swears by it.

machinery was oiled, the engines decoked. Lancashire laughter. It was another badge, another attitude to life. And for this new species, new heroes were needed to tell the world who Homo Northwestus was and what was happening here.

Today there are lots of people who are ashamed by the L. S. Lowry–George Formby–Blackpool image of the North-West. 'It's not what we are,' they say. 'The North-West has moved on.' But they forget that Homo Northwestus histori-cally has no heritage from which to choose. He has no heroes from days of yore. Rob Roy in his kilt was not a familiar figure in Rossendale, and when Robin Hood supped from a well above Helmshore he was almost certainly lost – or, worse . . . it was an imposter. It's also said that Joseph of Arimathea's twig was planted near Warrington, where it still flowers in Appleton Thorn, but the tribal inheritance of these parts is thin on rebel songs to sing, or airs to fiddle.

Instead, it was from cheap and cheerful Lancashire that the first post-industrial music hall turns came. These were to be the only real cultural concoction of Homo Northwestus, and the worst of it is . . . we only remember the gormless George . . .

On the first September weekend of every year, the latter-day custodians of Lancashire's cultural inheritance will gather in Fleetwood for a knees-up. The annual Fylde Folk Festival is more than a celebration, it's a jubilant affirmation that all those Lanky things of Emma Edge's young days do indeed still have their feverishly enthusiastic practitioners. In pubs rattled only by Fleetwood's infrequent Sunday trams, chubby men in white sweaters will gleefully jam a finger in one ear to belt out industrial Lancashire's greatest hits, eyes closed and pints gently rocking. Elsewhere there'll be earnestly-fought clog dancing competitions. The Rivington Ladies' Morris and the Bispham Barnstormers will give of their best and, in a bleak room above the public library, three silver pots stand in wait for the winners of a blue riband event.

The Lancashire Dialect Society exists for the preservation of the old county's native tongue. It has less than two hundred members

as of March 1991, but still 'the people of the 25th century will thank us for it,' claims society chairman Bob Dobson, an ex-policeman whose job it is to run their annual dialect poetry competition, one of the highlights of the Fleetwood gathering. Each of the three cups is fiercely contested, but last year, the thirteenth such Lanky Eisteddfod, it was the Eric Topping Trophy for humorous verse which, some say, drew the finest work.

△ Jim Atherton, poet.

For months the leading protagonists had been polishing their poems and their performances, and none more so than Darwen's Jim Atherton, whose piece, 'The Queen Street Mill Lament', had rightly earned him the Sam Laycock pot for more serious work in 1989. 'I'm not really very fond of proper poetry. It never seems to me to be about anything you can relate to. My poems are about things that people can understand,' he says.

Jim grew up in Darwen, where his grandparents worked in the mills, and where his parents frowned on any exaggerated use of dialect speech. 'You spoke it at school with your mates,' he says, 'because your mum might give you a good hiding for using dialect

The Queen Street Lament, by Jim Atherton

Clickety clack, clickety clack,
Theear I goo a'looking back
There wor a time when England's bread
Depended on yor ceawnty's thread
To every problem we hed a solution
We were t'king ot th'industrial revolution
But it seems to be we've lost eawr way
For they're clooasin Queen Street mill today.

Just thowt of it fair jowls mi yed
No clatter o clugs in t'weyvin shed
No 'Mee mawin' neaw across the alley
Just bailiff's knock and an empty bally
Aw t'coyles bin brunt we're deawn tut cinders
Eawr pride alas flown eawt ut windows
Monny geet deawn on their knees to pray
As they would'nd clooas Queen Street mill today.

Kissing t'shuttles gone for ever
So is picking sticks and t'smell o leather
No rhythmic thump from th'engine 'peace'
Or t'smell we knew fra oil and grease
Mon thad engine run as smooth as silk
But it's no use skrikin oer spilt milk
We're towd we's hev to ged on us way
When we've wovven t'last cut at mill today.

Nod only wor we weyvin cotton
We wove friendships neer to be forgotten
T'wer one for all and all for one
But we've coom tut th'end ut rooad by gum
It's no brass neaw lass in thi poss
No tekkin t'babby eawt to noss
But we's force a smile aye come what may
Though they're clooasin Queen Street mill today.

'Tis aysther [Easter] time, hark tut joyful seawnd
Rising up from t'valleys aw areawnd
Childther''s voices, men o brass
As yon aysther bells play yor requiem mass
We watch um as they wheel eawt beeams
'Cos they're wheeling eawt, aye aw eawr dreeams
It's last act of a drama that they play
As final curtain faws on t'mill today.

It's part of eawr heritage so they say
Why did we let it slip away?
Future generations never will forgive
The penny pinching way we live
Millions made yet nooan to spare
To show the world the way we were
There's brass for th'arts or so they say
But it's sorry, there's nowt for t'mill today.

TV crews coom and they filmed aw day
T'wer quiet when they went away
But yo con bet your Taiwan wovven socks
T'will be t'biggest tradgedy there's been on t'box
We's think as we hang up eawr clugs
Wod a shame to see t'mill go tut dugs
For we're in t'breykers' hands there's nowt mooar
    to say
Mon the devil's in yon mill today

Clickety clack, clickety clack, wer a musical
    seawnd
Whilst playing it put in eawr pockets a peawnd
But fate stopped eawr music, no mooar will it play
It's too late 'cos they clooased Queen Street mill
    yesterday.

expressions at home.' It was fifteen years ago that he came out of the dialect closet, reading a poem at a civic 'do' for the first time. Now he's a regular turn on the poetry circuit; a genuine character in clogs and cap who can raise a bob or two for charity, as well as hearty laughter at the schools, pubs and clubs he's repeatedly booked into.

'We consider ourselves missionaries. We're going abroad and spreading the gospel. I've been out 28 times this year throughout the county and the demand is there. But in order to make dialect more acceptable to people of today you've got to talk more about the subjects of today, so I've written about mad cow disease, poll tax, the Ceausescus . . .'

And so at Fleetwood on a September Sunday last year, Jim turned up with his latest poem about a man looking after himself while his wife recovered from illness in hospital:

I'd like to come and visit thee, but I've geet so much to do,
Pup's tail's just flown in't th'oover, and Lucinda's gettin t'flu.
I put rice krispies intut wesher, well t'packets aw looked the same.
Neaw they'r snap crackle poppin waw to waw and t'budgie's just gone
*   lame.*

Yor Jamie's down w t'mayzles, that's heaw mi story goes.
He's get mooar spots aw oer his chops, ner a set o dominoes
But dor'nd worry lass I'm copin, I'm usin two quarts tin
To try to catch aw t'wather for it's started rainin' in.

On the day it was read with all the verve and comic timing Jim could muster, but for the Eric Topping Trophy 1991 it just wasn't quite enough. It was a younger girl, a charismatic 14-year old called Rebecca Duggan, who held the pot aloft after reading the verse of her gifted grandmother, Doris Snape of Great Harwood:

Ah wor weshing' up inta t'kitchen las'neet,
Wi't sink full o'sooapy watter,
When t'dooar bustin' oppen gi' mi such a freet,
Ah sheawted, 'Good 'eavens! Wot's matter?'

Eawr Bert stood theer, 'is fore'ead aw red,
'Is face covered with slutch, snot and dust.
'Ee Albert wot's 'appened ta thee?' ah sed,
'An' stop scrykin' like thad or tha'll bust.'

'Dorned se that's bin fawin' deawn ageean!'
'Now ah 'evvened eawr Ethel,' 'e sed,
'Tha knows big Billy who lives ad sixteen?
Well, 'e shoved mi, an ah've banged m'o'ead.'

It's easy to walk away from these Lanky dos and pick on the inconsistencies; people glowing for the good old days which any close examination shows were *not* good. Far too often the dialect poets seem to be pickling a memory in the past, soaking it in some ancient tongue which is no longer spoken outside of dialect society meetings. The sounds of Homo Northwestus have changed constantly over the centuries, and phoneticists have even said his accent originally was from the Midlands. Imagine that. Homo Northwestus, a Brummie?

> 6 Far too often the dialect poets seem to be pickling a memory in the past, soaking it in some ancient tongue. 9

'Yes, we are preserving the past,' says Bob Dobson, whose own publishing company specialises in homespun Lancashire verse. 'But this is the language of Shakespeare and Chaucer. This is real England, the real English language. There are words here which have died out in standard English which have been preserved in little pockets like Lancashire. It's vitally important, wonderfully important, to keep them.'

Homo Northwestus, after all, likes the idea of being friendly – even the incomers do. He's also deeply nostalgic for the manner of his own backstreet past; for the smile, if not the grind, of work. That's why, at a dialect reading in a Bacup church hall, it will be older people mainly who come to hear Bob Dobson's latest discoveries. Rebecca Duggan won the Eric Topping Trophy, but she won it for her gran. There are not many teenagers on the dialect circuit, and if it's to survive beyond being sweetly sentimental it will be poets like Jim Atherton who carry the form forward. Because, in Jim's own words, 'It's a forceful medium which should be about present-day subjects if it's to appeal to present-day listeners'.

There were great poets of Lancashire once, who were as celebrated in the nineteenth century as much as the three Liverpool poets, Henri, Patten and McGough, were lauded in the 'sixties. Their work wasn't always just restricted to sugary, fireside rhyming platitudes. If roused they could, and did, pen the sort of angry protest poems which alerted middle-class southern audiences to the consequences of social disasters like the Cotton Famine. Just as Woody Guthrie's songs would later alert Washington to the dustbowl tragedy of Oklahoma farmers, so would the dialect poets highlight the unpredictable climate of Lancashire's milltowns. And back home they were so adored that the cemeteries of North-East Lancashire are dotted with monuments which today's dialect enthusiasts regard with the tenderness reserved for holy shrines.

In Rochdale Parish Churchyard is 'Tim Bobbin's' grave, where the remains of John Collier lie. Not John Collier the gents' outfitter (whose window was the one to watch), but John Collier the man regarded by some as the father of Lancashire dialect writing. 'Tim Bobbin' was his pseudonym and his enemies were the pompous and the pious. Even the doggerel on his weathered headstone hints at the irreverence of the character beneath it:

> *Here lies John and with him Mary*
> *Cheek by jowl and never vary*
> *No wonder that they so agree*
> *John wants no punch and Moll no tea*

In Queen's Park, Harpurhey, Manchester, another poet – Ben Brierley – was remembered by a monument and, nearby, by a pub which took his name. He'd been born in 1825 and found work at 't'loom' from the age of five. It was said that Ben, like many determined working-class Victorian intellectuals, had found for himself the joys of great literature. He read Shakespeare and Southey, and went into print first with the *Manchester Spectator*, his piece entitled 'A day out – or a summer ramble in Daisy Nook'. For 22 years he would produce his own weekly *Ben Brierley's Journal*, and 'set forth with great faithfulness and power the life of the working folk of Lancashire'.

> ❛ The cemeteries of North East Lancashire are dotted with monuments to the dialect poets. ❜

Samuel Bamford was another who coupled his radical views with poetry and became an influential figure, with a monument in Middleton Churchyard to his name. He'd worked a handloom in the town for most of his life, and organised the town's radicals into a club which he himself had led to the infamous affair at St. Peter's Field in 1819 – what we now call 'Peterloo'. Ben Brierley was among those who penned lines of tribute after Bamford's death in 1872. It took the form of a conversation in which Sam said:

> *I need no monument, not I*
> *Well not o'sculptured stone.*
> *Look i'my 'Radical' it's there –*
> *A tablet o'my own.*

But head and whiskers above them all was Edwin Waugh, a dialect poet whose work sold by the wagon-load and who still has a small but loyal society dedicated to the preservation of his art and the perpetuation of his name. They'll meet on the second Wednesday of every month at a United Reform Church in Smith Street, Rochdale (7.30 prompt) and each year on a warm summer Saturday it's likely you'll see the sprightliest members of the Edwin Waugh Dialect Society striding the West Pennine fells high above Edenfield.

They'll be heading to the supreme viewpoint of Waugh's Well, where tangy spring-water chatters into a stone trough beneath a stern bronze image of Waugh which looks uncannily like Karl Marx. It was here that the poet would sit and rest on his long moorland rambles and reflect, no doubt, on how fortunate he had been. Unlike Ben Brierley, Waugh never worked in the cotton trade and, although he cultivated a 'man of the people' persona, research shows he was anything but. Instead, Waugh was bookish and felt uncomfortable with the working people who enjoyed and purchased his work in such great quantity. In all they, and the London society hostesses who simply adored him, bought one million copies of his books. And while Waugh's critics say he damaged dialect verse and trivialised the penny-scraping poor who flocked

▽ A van advertising the location of a fish and chip shop in Colne. What kind of image do the poets try to portray . . . or create?

to buy his cheaper editions, there were still thousands lining the streets when his body was returned from New Brighton to Kersal for his funeral in 1890. 'Dialect writing had lost its cutting edge,' wrote one Waugh scholar. 'It became a source of solace rather than a critique of industrial society. It came to fit very comfortably into middle- class norms of morality and expectations.'

At the end of the great Victorian age the public had become tired of the dialect poets. The new political and social expectations of the century found no voice in a verse form which was already harking back to the golden never-never land so many poets still seem stuck in. Quickly it withdrew to the margins, where it survives today – like cows' udders and tripe – a faint shadow of an art form which had belonged entirely to Homo Northwestus. Through it the species had its own unique sense of community reinforced. No-one else could share in dialect poetry. The poems never travelled well, and because of that, as the species diluted, their resonance and purpose were lost. To most people in the modern North-West now, they are little more than a quaint eccentricity.

Roll up, roll up, see the tattooed lady.
See the lovely lady with the pictures on her skin.
In went the lads and they began to cheer, for there upon her back were all
*   the towns of Lancashire.*
There were Oswaldtwistle, Manchester city, the town hall standing in the
*   square, ta ra ra.*
Oldham, Bolton, Ashton-under-Lyne. The pitheads at Leigh were looking
*   mighty fine.*
When someone shouted 'Daddy, don't go down the mine,'
At the Rawtenstall Annual Fair.

Few songs can match 'The Rawtenstall Annual Fair' for its seemingly authentic and Brueghel-esque portrait of weekend life in a typical Lancashire town. As the 'lads' in it stagger from freak show to peep show – 'ee she were a big 'un with accent on the big' – they seem to have taken live form in a Lowry painting. It's a song which is also enormously popular with ethnic folkies, a regular at 'singers' night', and easy to remember after the heaviest of evenings. As soon as he hears it, the Mike Harding in every Homo Northwestus purrs while the other half shuts his ears, embarrassed to hear such old-time tripe.

But for all that, 'Rawtenstall Annual Fair' was written by a couple of pearly queens from London, Lee and Weston, for a Cockney comic called Randolph Sutton whose act was to mock hapless, harmless, pie-eating folk from the music hall and hippodrome fleapits he played. By accident, Homo Northwestus has taken up as his own what was really someone else taking the mickey – as many still do. Homo Northwestus had made a simple culture out of smiling at misfortune, or laughing at himself. But when he had stopped, the world carried on laughing at Lancashire and many members of the species are embarrassed.

Perhaps that's why you won't find much of Emma Edge's old Lancashire in the county's most prestigious magazine, *Lancashire Life*, which is put together in Preston for the thirteen readers who are said to look at every copy sold. In dentists' receptions throughout the North-West, Homo Northwestus will pick one up and wonder why it is that in *Lancashire Life* everything looks so much like Cheshire.

Take the New Year edition for 1992 as an example. There are far more adverts for mobile phones and fitted fireplaces than there are for Padiham's finest cow heel. And if you're looking for an authentic Lancashire home, there's a snip of a Georgian parsonage at £375,000 but not so many mid-terraced homes 'in need of attention'. There's a feature on the Algarve; the new £20,000 Rover is tested; and at the BUPA Hospital Ball in Manchester, Miss Judith Evans and Mrs. Barbara Spragg are clearly having a marvellous time.

Since last year the dialect poetry corner has been dropped ('dialect poems on the Gulf War just didn't seem right'), and although there is nothing wrong with this – *Lancashire Life* is ready to identify and pursue its target market – there are voices which say it misrepresents what Lancashire stands for. Or what it did stand for, once. Voices like Bob Dobson's, who'll steadfastly argue: 'I don't think it's Lancashire at all. It only represents a very small minority of the people. The people of Lancashire are in the main much more working-class, down-to-earth and living in ordinary houses than, sadly, *Lancashire Life* might think. If it were my magazine I would have it represent a far truer picture of Lancashire than that small number of people who want to look at fancy adverts and fancy kitchens. Lancashire people aren't really interested in that.'

But they are. Because when *Lancashire Life* editor Brian Hargreaves mischievously profiles his typical reader it sounds a thousand light years from the George Formby of the films: 'I think it's somebody who lives outside a town or city in a nice detached house with a bit of ground and who goes to work in a Jag or BMW'.

'And that's Lancashire?' asks Ray.

'Yes, that's maybe one Lancashire. The sort of Lancashire that most of our readers belong to.'

'Has that Lancashire got anything to do with flat caps and tripe and George Formby and Cannon and Ball's braces?'

'Tripe,' says Brian with the hint of a smile, 'is very popular in the most expensive restaurants in Lancashire these days. Pigs' trotters and cow heels are part of that new style of cooking, and flat caps I think you find mainly on the best golf courses and grouse moors.'

It's not surprising that in this new-blooded entrepreneurial North-West a dialect poem about Saddam Hussein would go down in Brian's magazine like a cold cow's udder. And, although Bob Dobson may not like it, you can see Brian's point. How many race whippets? How many recite the Lord's Prayer the Lanky way? Not enough to keep *Lancashire Life* alive; and its readers are, increasingly, younger, wealthier and female.

> ' Tripe is very popular in the most expensive restaurants in Lancashire these days, along with cowheel and pigs' trotters. '

The Lancashire life this chapter is pursuing is the one we're really known for. It's Coronation Street in black and white – but even that has changed. Today you'll find Tracey and Sally and Raquel, and the front doors of the Rover's now swing open on to a row of modern houses whose occupants won't have a flat cap between them.

That Lancashire of Alf and Ena has had its borders messed about with more than the old Soviet Union; and who's called 'Alf' and 'Ena' today? To the people who remember it, Lancashire was a precious thing, and the soul of its tribe, Homo Northwestus, was special. Is it a different people today? Different from when the mill was 'nobbut a clog-hop away'; when Liverpool dockers were together in the same shed? The same shed, the same songs, the same poems, from the inner city to the robust industrial villages. Back then, Emma Edge will say, it was one culture, and when the whistle blew the whole lot went on holiday to the same place.

Homo Northwestus invented the seaside. Fish and chips, the naughty postcard, the seaside holiday. An entire way of life was his culture, work and play, that now cannot be but a shadow of what it was. Where the buses for Blackpool once queued in Bolton for

Wakes Weeks

'The Wakes Week was great. Everybody used to set off. Mother, father, grannies, aunties, uncles. Everybody went on the train. As a little girl it was the only place you went – Blackpool – and I used to be so terrified of the noise of the trains.

Grandma used to bake everything. She used to spend two days baking to fill the hampers and when you got there, to Blackpool, you went to Mrs. Cook's on Cook Street and it used to cost two and sixpence for your bed and a sixpence for the cruet. You used to give her all your food and she'd cook it for you. When you got to the end of the week you were broke so you'd get down to jam, bread and cornflakes . . .

The towns were dead because the mills closed for two weeks and all the tattlers and oilers and all the loom sweepers set off with their little suitcases and went on the train which took two hours because it stopped at every station . . . it was the highlight of your year and wherever you went there'd be somebody from your town there . . . Families don't live next door to one another like they used to do. They live in different towns and work in different places. When I was a girl everyone lived in the same street so that grandmother could look after the babies and make dinner for all the family who worked in the mills.'

Margaret Helliwell, dialect poet.

Wakes Weeks trips, now scores of little travel agents dish out packages to everywhere at any time of year. Back then, the cheap, familiar accommodation of countless Blackpool land-ladies would welcome the same families back, year after year, generation upon generation. United at home by work, pub and chapel, Homo Northwestus was now thrown together in play. And so rigid were the codes of his working life that in Blackpool the promenade would fall silent at mealtimes as Homo Northwestus retreated to his digs just when the lunchbreak whistle would have sounded in the mill.

By day, Homo Northwestus would enjoy the 'health-giving properties' of pre-EEC, pre-pollution bathing beaches, and by night he'd spend his hard-saved sixpences watching Marie Lloyd or Caruso at the best of the summer's pier shows. Florrie Forde was there, and Tom Mix. W. C. Fields juggled, and Blondin performed the penultimate tightrope walk of his life, falling off before Homo Northwestus's very eyes in 1895. There were Charlie Chaplin, Houdini, Dietrich, Noel Coward, even Sarah Bern-hardt, who so disappointed her audience that they booed and demanded their money back.

Blackpool is still immensely popular, as the M6 motorway queues prove well after most resorts have shuttered up for winter. But as Lancashire has changed and grown ever more cosmopolitan, so has the look of the crowds who swarm around the pleasure beach every summer weekend. Whole street-loads from Bacup no longer tumble out at Blackpool station. Today it is smaller groups, families or mid-sized works parties, for whom Blackpool is a cultural icon; a multi-coloured, tasteless fantasy where the vinegar and fried onions are only overpowered by the scent of salt-sea during the worst of weather; where the fancy

goods emporia will always stock plastic snot and mucky pup poos;
and where Bobby Ball's braces will glow forever brightly. And yet
Blackpool has changed. No longer is it the complete community
experience it once was. Those old industries are dead, their streets
breaking up. Only the ghosts of times past remain, their last
whispers tape-recorded and filed by a librarian from Rising Bridge.

Benita Moore collects people. At her home (not far from
the Hollands pie factory at Baxenden) she's got literally
hundreds of them; from the man who once shod Mussolini's horse,
to old Jimmy Stephenson who ran Ossie's potato pie shop in
Oswaldtwistle; from Arthur Crabtree, the
Stacksteads grocer, to Clarrie Greenwood, the
cheese stall man from Accrington market.
They don't live with her; not in person
anyway. Although she can energetically and
endlessly reel off the family trees of authen-
tically venerable Lancashire folk, these are not
real house guests. Not Joe or Annie. Nor
Agnes or Emma. These people are collected
on tapes, lovingly and magnetically stored on
the five hundred cassettes Benita has recorded during a lifetime's
romance with Homo Northwestus.

> 6 Lancashire means
> everything to me. It means
> my home people, my
> heritage . . . it's the best
> place on earth. 9

It began when she worked out of Ramsbottom with the county's

△ Benita Moore, tape
recorder at the ready.
She collects people.

mobile library service and, like most love affairs, it has been passionate, intense and untypically prolonged. 'Lancashire,' she says, 'means everything to me. It means my home, my people, my heritage . . . It's the best place on earth. I wouldn't like to be anywhere else at all. Lancashire people have special qualities. They're good-hearted and kind and have a strong sense of humour which in my books I've tried to portray.'

As she travelled around, dispensing books to the cheery occupants of countless two-up two-downs, Benita was introduced to dozens of the people who, in her eyes, best embodied this spirit. Here was an entire generation, thought Benita, who had made no great mark on the world as individuals, but who, together, recalled a fast-fading way of life. 'I wasn't so much interested in the dialect,' she says, 'it was the stories and the people themselves. If we don't collect these experiences they'll be lost forever.'

And so Benita equipped herself with a tape recorder and embarked on a missionary safari into the shifting sands of post-industrial Lancashire. Meeting little resistance at the door, she recorded – and still does – up to 25 hours of chat a week, tirelessly winkling out memories from her sometimes bemused victims.

'What about your Freddie? When you got married, did you go to Morecambe with him as well?', she asks Emma Edge.

'Yes. When we got married we did, and then we started going to Colwyn Bay.'

'Oh. Did you like it better there?'

'Yes, we did.'

'Why is that?'

'I don't know. We used to stop at a holiday home and, ee, you know, it were grand. It were real nice there at Colwyn Bay.'

'Was it a Methodist holiday home, Emma?'

'No, it were a friendship home they called it, but they always had a little service at night. Now wait a minute while I fetch some cups.'

Benita, as you would expect in a Lancashire romance, is faithful to the objects of her affection. The books she writes, and has published, are sentimental but usually unedited transcriptions of her fireside natters with anyone from a clogmaker to a corner shop-keeper. She does not tamper with their anecdotes, and her latest volume again attempts to capture, in their own words, the recollections of people near the end of their lives. Men like Brian Daley, who danced with Bacup's legendary coconutters for 29 years. Women like Maggie Edwards, who recalled the seaside holidays where she took the food – 'three eggs, butter, a tin of salmon, two tins of fruit and some cheese' – and the landlady cooked it. Alas, some of Benita's people have already gone. And although there are those who sniff at her hobby – saying she is unscientific, not a trained social historian – who else would have preserved them?

This is the old Lancashire, and it has no glossy magazine dedicated to the social musterings of its élite and glamorous. But for all that, is there still something here that cannot quite be extinguished? Did that old Lancashire hold something, despite its poverty, that was universally recognised; a pride in its separate togetherness which proved you could come out on top with a grin? For a moment, was Homo Northwestus a cultural rôle model for the world . . .?

I f your nose clears suddenly in a Wigan brick-built back-street on a still summer's day, there's a reason. If you then smell the sweet draught of peppermint, or the warm wind of bubbling syrup, look for the works chimney and the sign which reads: 'Uncle Joe's'. You can only be in one place: Dorning Street, Wigan, the home of the mint ball. With a little pre-planning you will be invited into the factory, where the glorious vapours and the time-locked manufacturing process will intoxicate and intrigue you. An enormous snake of shining mixture is massaged and folded, stretched and rolled. Young women, their hair tied neatly back, load wrapping machines with the sweet amber bullets which are still loyally sucked by customers around the globe. Mint balls. They're a legend; a folk song sung by Mike Harding; a triumph of *double entendre*; a crucial cornerstone in the Wigan myth: but in this story the sweets themselves hardly matter.

It's interesting to know how Ellen Seddon, Mrs. William Santus, first made toffee in her back kitchen to be sold on her husband's fruit stall almost one hundred years ago. It's astonishing to learn how popular they were with chesty miners and how, in 1919, Mr. Santus built the present sweet factory for nearly £2,500. It's touching to learn how his descendants today – John and Anthony Winnard – mix Fourths cane sugar and oil of American peppermint in secret proportions after the workforce have left each

Although there was no Uncle Joe, it seems likely that there was a 'Joe' of some sort. William Santus set up the company much as it is today, but it was his wife who boiled up the first sweets. She'd been friendly with another Wigan family, the Attys, who were well known locally for their multi-coloured mints, and it's believed that Mrs. Santus invented her own peppermint sweet to compete with them. Perhaps as a gesture of conciliation, they named their new confection after the Attys' son, Joe. Whatever the truth, Uncle Joe has survived, and his mints are made using processes and machinery almost 75 years old. At the last count, the Dorning Street factory's 32 staff were producing 125 tons of mint balls a year . . .

△ The distinctive Uncle Joe's advert painted onto the factory building in Wigan. It's seen by everyone as they travel on the main north-south railway.

◁ An Uncle Joe's employee working a large lump of the sticky mint ball mixture on a water-cooled slab.

night. But what really matters here is Uncle Joe. *Uncle* Joe. More friendly, somehow, than Colonel Sanders. More endearing, undoubtedly, than any Ronald McDonald. Even when we discover that he never really existed, he lives in spirit, as Homo Northwestus incarnate. Boiled sweets from a fond relative, offered in a sticky bag from an open door, its front step donkey-stoned and the kettle singing on the range . . . wait a minute while I fetch some cups.

It's that image others have of Lancashire again, and the closer you get, the better it seems. Uncle Joe is a marketing device and the

Santus family are not alone in seeing its power. Unscrupulous competitors have tried to muscle in with names like 'Uncle Bob's', or 'Grandpa Sam's' and Uncle Joe has had to see them off, the lot of them. History, too, is rapping at the Dorning Street door. In an age of pre-packed, multi-national sweetie giants, how many people still turn their pockets inside-out to find a half-sucked sherbet lemon or a forgotten floral gum? Just like the dialect poets and tripe dressers, Uncle Joe now clings voraciously to the nostalgia and leisure industries which so cleverly re-invent the past. Look closely and there he is, smiling down from his eye-catching red tins at Wigan Pier or Granada Studio Tours.

Suck the mint ball too hard, however, and it'll have your teeth. Play the dialect part too loud, or too often, and it's a stereotype just like George Formby's or Andy Kershaw's accent. People wince and turn away. They don't see that on the tongue of old Homo Northwestus was a spirit of such sweet goodness that it was universally recognised at the end of every pier and TV tube.

However Homo Northwestus today – the new breed – markets the past, he shouldn't apologise for it. It's all he's got. In the rush to erect a new North-West, he should take time not to discard or dismiss those parts of the past the species thinks it's outgrown.

△ Street corner society in Bacup, Lancashire.

The vitality of community and self-help were qualities elevated by the dialect poets and, for Homo Northwestus, within still-living memory, became central to his view of himself and his fellow man.

Sharing and helping would give us, from Rochdale, the Co-operative Movement. Bluff, straight-talking honesty would give us the foundation of radical journalism in the *Manchester Guardian*. And those closest to the secret recipe of this now-diminished Lancashire culture would go on to become the region's greatest heroes.

Chapter FOUR | A statue in the park

EVERY trophy in the cupboard, Homo Northwestus has won. Near as damn it he invented the football, and the greatest teams of the English divisions have been ours. From Accrington Stanley to Preston North End. Not just the giants who survive today, but little teams, forgotten stars, whose cork studs proudly graced the fields and pitches of towns like Darwen who, in 1883, still had three sides in the draw for the second round of the FA Cup.

Great heroes have made it from these pitches of Lancashire on to cigarette cards and the covers of magazines; but are there greater heroes of the North-West whose stature is measured by more than the weight of a pass? Not just sporting legends – we could fill the book with them – but real contributors on the field of life? Who today can Homo Northwestus admire, if anyone, as one of his own; a person of these parts who has made good and stayed true to something more than just fame; a person whose statue really would belong in every park?

You see, in the past, even before Bryan Robson's first groin strain, the North-West has had no ancient folk hero to bind him together. Unlike the Welsh, unlike the East Anglians, Homo Northwestus has had no Prince Llewellwyn, no Hereward the Wake, no Queen Boadicea. It is true that Butch Cassidy's dad was a Preston Mormon, but Butch was born in Utah and, unlike Robin Hood, he hardly ever gave to the poor. In any case, Butch spoke the Yankee way, not the Lanky way and, no matter where you look, it's not until the football age of industry and terraces that Homo Northwestus gets heroes. So who might they be?

Cilla Black, our Maid Marian? Dr. Steptoe and his many test-tube sons of Oldham? Sean Ryder, of Happy Mondays; or Anthony Burgess, the writer? Maybe it's Cyril Smith, our Friar Tuck? Eddie Shah, our Sheriff of Nottingham? Derek Hatton? Joe Bloggs? How can we distinguish between celebrities like Jim Bowen and those real heroes who did good, or changed us, and never asked for a fee? Or, like the song, is it: No more heroes any more?

Pat Seed, perhaps; dying of cancer and raising money to help others, even as her husband was tragically killed at the Abbeystead pumping station disaster near Lancaster in 1984? Elsie Tanner, the same? Brave, battling, an inspiration for independent working women. Or Eileen Bilton saying, 'Give us a ring,' in Warrington New Town? Yosser? The man who grasped *the* question for the '80s and '90s: 'Give us a job'.

The truth is that it takes time to join the elect. Real heroes have staying power and no-one can yet know what names future generations will automatically inherit as the great figures of our day. In the hall of fame no heroes are secure. Every era has its favourites, so, in fifty years' time, will there be 'Happy Mondays' impersonators in every Friday night pub talent contest?

Once it was Gracie Fields, not Sean Ryder, who was No. 1 for the big-boned embodiment of Lancashire; the very spirit of warm-hearted, friendly backstreets – although she wasn't living in one, and hadn't been for years. Our Gracie, she was then; forever returning to Rochdale to meet the Mayor and wave to the crowds from the town hall steps. In the North-West Film Archive at Manchester Polytechnic you can watch her returning time after time, year on year, in her full-length dark coat with its sensible fur collar. She'd married an Italian, Boris, and lived on the Isle of Capri, off Naples (in voluntary exile, like the Emperor Tiberius) hoping we'd think she'd not forgotten us when, in reality, we were forgetting her.

Gracie had been born Grace Stansfield in 1898, and her saccharin cheeriness had sugared the Depression for millions. And although it wasn't the finest voice, her songs did celebrate that great, mythical northern stoicism to which Homo Northwestus felt he could naturally subscribe. He had, after all, been bashed for so long that a champion who could 'Look on the Bright Side' (1931), or 'Look Up and Laugh' (1935) seemed well worth the price of a ticket to the Winter

WILLS'S CIGARETTES

GRACIE FIELDS

6 Gracie Fields seemed to be the embodiment of the spirit of warm-hearted, friendly Lancashire. 9

Gardens. Her autobiography was called *Sing As We Go*, but when it was published the singing had long stopped and Gracie had long gone. He's always rewarded local loyalty, has Homo Northwestus and, for however long Gracie lingers in the communal heart, she can never match George Formby, who stayed. Just like Rochdale's Stansfield for the 'nineties, Lisa, says she will.

So many did make their packet and push off. In Liverpool, until recently, people would say, 'What did The Beatles ever do for Liverpool once they'd made it?' For so many it seemed the first acquisition was a detached home in the Home Counties with a white Rolls Royce and a white piano. John Lennon? He grew up in Menlove Avenue, Liverpool but, in our heads, was he not mostly in New York? Professional northerners abounded in the 'sixties; international curiosities, cocktail celebrities who wore their quaint, industrial, bog-soaked roots like a sponsor's motif.

And George Formby? Alone and unaided, he spawned an image and an industry that simply grows and grows. Poor, fur-wrapped Gracie. She'll never have what George has now; a worldwide society with nine hundred members from Stockholm to Sydney, Paisley to Peking, every one of them capable of picking a uke and humming every last daft line ever spun by goofy old, toothy old Mr. Wu. Three times a year they'll gather at the Winter Gardens in Blackpool to sing, every nostril pinched in a massed nasal rendering of Formby's finest follies. It's a phenomenon. It's frightening. Even George Harrison is a fan.

△ What did the Beatles ever do for the North-West once they'd made it?

Formby's father had started it all. He was billed as 'The Wigan Nightingale', and his catchphrase drew a cackle from the bronchial sputum which filled the lungs of music-hall audiences. 'Coughing better tonight,' he'd splutter, until his own fatal coughing spasm in 1921 brought the final curtain down on George Senior's less than illustrious showbusiness career. It was an age when Homo Northwestus could raise a laugh about his own chronic ill-health, just as Gracie and George could pack the cinemas with jolly tales of unemployed life and breadline poverty.

It was *Off the Dole* in 1934 which launched Formby Junior as pure box-office gold. Can you imagine a musical comedy today on the plight of redundant miners, or unemployed steelworkers? And yet *Off the Dole* helped launch the artless Formby, at the age of 29, into an unruffled silver sea of cinematic success. Homo Northwestus could never tire of George, it seemed, and as hit piled on hit, the ivory smile shone brighter and bigger. And, of course, he'd stayed here, true to the tribe. From backstreet Wigan he'd progressed to the Promenade at Fairhaven, where he lived with his wife Beryl, to all their devoted world its most devoted couple. But not so.

It was said that Beryl had spotted George in the '20s and masterminded his every move, as did Tom Parker with Elvis and Brian Epstein with the early Beatles. She had married and suppressed him; calling him for meals with a police whistle, seeing off female fans, and restricting Britain's biggest box-office draw to a daily allowance of 25p. It was all the very stuff of McGill's seaside postcards, the gormless, hen-pecked buffoon and his overpowering wife – from whom George, in the end, almost escaped. She'd died at Christmas in 1960 and Formby, now his secret life was seeping out, planned to marry again. Alas, he died in March the following year. It had nearly turned out nice at last, but not quite.

PLAYER'S CIGARETTES

George Formby

GEORGE FORMBY

△ Alone and unaided he spawned an industry which grows and grows.

It isn't easy to become a hero and get your statue in the park. You can't become a hero simply by hiring an agent and making a pot of money. Many try and some succeed – you'll have seen them on Wogan – but to Homo Northwestus a hero is much more than a celebrity. And those heroes who are elevated in their own lands often tell us a great deal about the qualities most admired by each particular species. So, to the Welsh, Dylan Thomas and Richard Burton for their passion and love of the language; so, to the Scots, Sean Connery, Kenny Dalglish, Billy Connelly, each one a hard, dry man from a race of survivors. And the Irish? Look to Brendan Behan, even Bob Geldof; living, thinking, hard-dreaming people, poets and pint-pot philosophers.

These heroes reflect back on each distinct species and tell us what they most admire; and if that's true for nations like Scotland and Wales, what of smaller sub-states like Lancashire? Who is it that Homo Northwestus would choose? Ask the world and it will reply, 'George Formby'. But is that the best we can do? A fond fool, a smutty song, an enormous set of marble teeth?

One hundred years ago we'd have had no trouble naming our

heroic Homo Northwestus. Labour, Liberal or Conservative, Catholic, Protestant or Jew, all could agree and subscribe to a statue in the park. These would be reformers or benefactors, strivers for wealth and the betterment of this downtrodden species. Men with sideburns and frock coats who, by public subscription – or a discreet clause in a will – left their likenesses chipped in creamy marble. Politicians and princes who glower for all time from polished granite pedestals throughout our civic North-West. But what of the ordinary Joe? The unknown soldier whose battles ennobled the life of Homo Northwestus, but who won no elections and made no great uplifting speeches?

Sometimes they can be found. Under the green canopy of overgrown Wigan Cemetery is the grave of miners' leader William Pickard, whose headstone was paid for by 35,000 Lancashire miners. He'd won one thousand Labour votes during the 1874 General Election. He'd worked as a miner from eight years old, pulling coal from a Blackrod mine. He'd fought, as a miners' official, for improved safety, and those at his funeral in 1887 heard him described as 'the beau-ideal of the miners' agent . . . we shall seldom see his like again'. And yet there is nothing startling in William Pickard's life. It appears in no standard history of our species. Only those who stumble across his grave will ever encounter his name, but surely here Homo Northwestus has an authentic hero.

As it does in J. T. Fielding, whose own statue was unveiled in Queen's Park, Bolton, in the presence of over 100,000 people. It was by merging two textile unions into the giant Operative Cotton Spinners' Association that Fielding wielded power, using his nimble brain to pick through the wages minefield of an industry that dominated his town, and every other town in north-east Lancashire. Like Pickard, Fielding was mourned in style. His funeral was such 'as surely never before in the history of the town had been afforded a working man'. Two years later, in 1896, it was an aristocrat, Lord James of Hereford, who pulled away the veil from his monument.

Homo Northwestus had had nothing. For so long his had been the 38th out of the 38 counties and when some single individual helped to free him from the bogs of time he was thankful. Of course he was. Kings and emperors had passed him by and here, finally, in his greatest century, an outstretched hand was offering work, security and a place in history. One hundred years ago it wasn't easy to get your statue in the park, but there was no trouble identifying those who deserved one. They were union officials and miners' leaders mostly, not pop stars or footballers, but still it was the big men mostly who took their place on the public plinth. Most likely it would be the all-round entrepreneuring hero who'd start out poor, one of the lads, and have a bright idea which worked. He'd make pots of money and rise to fame and power with which this heroic man might practise philanthropy, and improve the world through his effort.

William Lever was, by any measure, a North-West hero. By his own bootstraps he'd pulled himself up from a Bolton backstreet to become a god whose workers cheered him from Birkenhead to the Belgian Congo. All it had taken was a simple idea and there he was; a Liberal MP, a Viscount, a millionaire, a patron of the arts and a Lanky lad with a fierce loyalty to the tribe.

He'd sold groceries as a young man and tripped four times to the church on Sundays at the side of his devout, non-smoking, non-drinking father. These were fastidious times. However dark their thoughts were, the Victorians required scrupulously scrubbed bodies and 200,000 tons of soap were sold annually to keep them so. It was an unappealing product upon which to build a legend, but Lever was a shrewd and unromantic man. Before him, the soap had been cut from fatty, crumbling blocks like cheese. By pre-cutting, wrapping and calling it 'Sunlight', Lever's fortune was assured.

▽ Lord Leverhulme's contribution to modern society was to package soap neatly . . . and he made a fortune on it.

But it was how he ran his blossoming business that was to elevate Lever in the heart of Homo Northwestus. By situating his works on the Wirral and by housing his 3,500 employees in the model conditions of Port Sunlight, Lever demonstrated a compassion only the most enlightened of entrepreneurs had shown before him. Cynical it may have been – his happy workers increased soap production by 1,500% in just ten years – but the schools and leisure facilities, the works trips to Paris, inspired genuine loyalty and affection. Remember again, the Romans had passed Homo Northwestus by. So many who should have enabled him to climb the ladder had exploited what few resources the North-West had. Lever, like Pickard and Fielding, held out the rare offer of a leg up. No wonder he got his statue in the park.

But Homo Northwestus was changing. Although Lever had lifted his lucky ones out of the slums and placed them in mock-Tudor terraces, it was Lever himself who still pulled every string of their lives. And once they'd paid their debt in the factory they didn't want his proposed daily two hours of physical training. After the First World War they no longer relished the ascetic social vision of a man who slept on his manor house roof and who, as an indirect consequence, died of pneumonia in May 1925.

Lever's body was laid in state at the Port Sunlight Art Gallery, itself dedicated to the memory of his Bolton-born wife. He'd been one of us, had Bill, and although the Sunlighters who streamed past his body now dismissed his oppressive paternalism, Lever had broken the mould, thrown away the stovepipe hat, set new standards others would emulate. He'd worked hard, stayed in Lancashire, and spoken his mind. He went to church, and when his workers did well he gave each a copy of a book which he'd read and which inspired him as it was later to inspire Mrs. Thatcher: *Self-Help* by Samuel Smiles; a DIY guide to business success.

Who today does Homo Northwestus have of that stature to admire? John Moores of Littlewoods Pools? Eddie Shah? Owen Oyston? Perhaps not. Indeed, it was said even a hundred years ago (by the man who created Sherlock Holmes) that Lancashire had the lowest number of eminent people in all England. Conan Doyle, we now know, was quite, quite wrong. He should have known better, taught by Lancashire Jesuits at Stonyhurst. Because when opportunity knocked – as it had around Sir Arthur's time – Homo Northwestus had proved himself anything but lacking in the necessary to improve the world. At a stroke, from wherever he'd come, Homo Northwestus had more than enough stuff of which statues are put up in parks.

It was an Accrington man, Wallace Hartley, who led the band into the icy ocean when the *Titanic* sank in 1912.

It was a Colne man, another Hartley, who gave the world its finest jam.

It was Lancashire's own Alcock and Brown who flew over the Atlantic and into a Connemara bog.

It was Salford that beat London with gas street lamps, in Chapel Street.

It was Blackpool that beat all with its electric trams in 1885.

The world's first computer was in Manchester, and it was in Lancashire, too, that the atom was split.

Richmal Crompton was from Bury . . . Alistair Cooke went to Blackpool Grammar . . . the author of *Little Lord Fauntleroy*, Frances Hodgson Burnett, was a Cheetham Hill shopkeeper's daughter . . . Ted Ray . . . Arthur Askey . . . Tommy Handley . . . Homo Northwestus all.

Henry Tate, a grocer's boy from Chorley, invented the sugar cube. The cure for constipation from New York to New Brighton was 'Dr. Beecham' of Wigan and St. Helens. Edmund Wrigley, of Delph, went to America and sent back chewing gum. Wherever you look, whenever you look, Conan Doyle was wrong, wrong, wrong. The North-West was top of the premier league, not just for Butch Cassidy, but the Ewbank sweeper, pioneered in Accrington . . . and the submarine, thought up first by a corrupt curate from Manchester's Moss Side.

But for the curiosity of his biographer, William Murphy, the world would have lost the Reverend George Garrett Pasha and his quixotic, doomed life of calamity. As it is there is no statue in the

WILLS'S CIGARETTES

TOMMY HANDLEY

△ George Garrett Pasha (the one with his hand on his heart) finally tired of life in 1902, a pauper with 66 cents in his pocket.

◁ Pasha with his 'flying saucer of the seas'. Surely one of the North-West's most heroic failures? It is rumoured that some enthusiasts have plans to rescue this pioneering craft from the bottom of the Irish Sea.

park, and even the Garrett family plaque at the reconstructed Christ Church, Moss Side, chooses to ignore his contribution to military science.

Perhaps that's because Garrett and his father, also a churchman, had systematically plundered the collecting box in order to pursue George's unlikely underwater fantasy. And, years later, when the barmy bubble had burst and Garrett's father died suddenly at the pulpit during a sermon about sudden death, there were doubtless those in Moss Side who felt that justice had been done. By then it was certainly too late to retrieve the embezzled funds anyway.

Garrett junior had gone on to design and build the world's first powered submarine. He'd christened it *Resurgam*, 'I shall rise again', and skippered it proudly out of Liverpool in 1880. But this flying saucer of the seas was a deathtrap. The temperatures inside climbed to 85° and, when the hatch was left open during a storm off Colwyn Bay, it sank, no hands lost. Unperturbed, he took his blueprints to the Turkish fleet where the navy's patience ran out with a £2,000 golden handshake from the Imperial Ottoman Bank . . . which bounced.

And George? He turned up in the United States – growing rice, fighting in the American–Spanish war, but tired of submarines and, finally tiring of life in 1902, a pauper with just 66 cents to his name. It's said that there are plans to bring the *Resurgam* back from the bottom of the Irish Sea, to give Garrett overdue credit for his contribution to naval warfare. Far too often, we forget our triers.

Poor John Osbaldeston had tried. He'd invented the weft fork which stopped the thrumming looms when the thread snapped. But in drunken conversations he'd given his secret away and, while others grew richer by his brainwave, poor John did not. 'Others have fattened and are still fattening upon the products of my exertions,' he wrote. 'My fault has been poverty, my weakness has been that I did not rank with the great.' He died at the workhouse in 1862, a broken man who left only the instructions for his Tockholes headstone: 'Here lies John Osbaldeston, a humble inventor, who raised many to wealth and fortune but himself lived in poverty and died in obscurity, the dupe of false friends and the victim of misplaced confidence.'

We forget the big men, too. In the hall of fame no heroes are secure. Of the millions who drive up the M6, it's only a very few who know what the temple on the hill is to commemorate as you take the curve east of Lancaster. Those façades of Portland stone, those balustrades of Cornish granite were built when, and for whom? And even in the city itself there will be those who know its name – the Ashton Memorial – but not one fact about the man who built or the woman who inspired it.

Lancaster, one hundred years ago, was Lord Ashton's town. His father, James Williamson, had started a successful linoleum business which his son inherited and built up until one in four of the city's adult population drew their pay from him. He was town councillor, High Sheriff, JP, MP and, from 1895, Baron Ashton of Ashton, Lord Lino of Lancaster – a man who would never pose for a single photograph in his life.

He spent over £400,000 on Lancaster and Morecambe, building a new town hall, a new wing for the lunatic asylum and, in

1909, for £87,000, what Pevsner would call 'the grandest monument,' a 'poem in stone,' the most dazzling folly in all Lancashire. The memorial, it was said, was built to the memory of his second wife, Jessie, but by completion in 1909 Ashton had married again, and today the dedication plaque is pledged coyly to all his family.

But, like Osbaldeston, and unlike Leverhulme, Ashton was to die in almost complete obscurity, the affection of his people squandered and abused. In almost everything Ashton did you can detect the self-aggrandising egocentricity of a man with his eyes on posterity, whose instincts lay with himself, not with his workforce. Leverhulme was no saint but, as Labour politics gripped northern workers, he could never have written the open letter Ashton fired off to his own employees as Liberal fortunes in Lancaster faded: 'I regret very much that some of the workpeople have unfortunately become disloyal and discontented owing to their having too readily listened to the bad advice of their fellow workmen and one or two outsiders.'

For the town and its benefactor it was the final straw. Ashton withdrew to shuttle between St. Annes and his residence at Ryelands, where his hours often passed in the saddle of a trick cycle on a specially laid-out track behind the high perimeter walls.

△ The temple on the hill . . . of the millions who drive past Lancaster on the M6, how many know what it is?

Within ten years of completion, his memorial was already in need of repairs, which Ashton himself was obliged to fund. By 1981, family ties with the city long gone, the City Architect found it so unsafe he was forced to close it to the public.

Ashton has his park (he provided it himself), but in it there is no statue. That subtle chemistry between Homo Northwestus and his first industrial heroes is absent in Lancaster. Even though the city's tourist literature steps discreetly round Lord Lino's less savoury moments, the sense of lingering unpopularity remains. Making a pot of money and ploughing some of it back isn't enough unless it is done with love. Homo Northwestus is a caring species and expects those virtues in all, however elevated they may think they are.

> **Making a pot of money and ploughing some of it back isn't enough unless it's done with love.**

△ More Alberts in the park than Victorias.

Whatever the truth often is of these old Victorian industrialists, however, they are lasting longer as monuments and statues in the park than old Joe Stalin in Russia. Williamson Park and the Ashton Memorial have not been renamed. The mobs haven't run up from Dalton Square in Lancaster and burned it down. Perhaps, in this case, it's because it's dedicated to a woman; and in the story of Homo Northwestus maybe women are more important than anywhere else in the land. Some might argue that Lancashire even invented women.

And yet how many statues in the park are female? Very few. It's true that Gracie has a bust and a theatre in Rochdale, but in Manchester there are surely more Alberts than Victorias. And if you had to name just three heroes for desert island Homo Northwestus-discus they could not all be men. There would have to be two women at least.

Hilda. Elsie. Ena. Cilla. Emmeline. Christabel. Mrs. Gaskell. Barbara Castle. Victoria Wood. Eileen Bilton. Dora Bryan. Bessie Braddock. Lisa. Gracie. Bet.

The very idea of a strong, earning woman was the product of our industrial revolution. Homo Northwestus had stepped out of the bog with his women at the loom or down the mine, and throughout the nineteenth century the numbers of working women, particularly in cotton, continued to climb. It was no accident that the movement which culminated in votes for women found its first voice in Lancashire. The Pankhursts may have relocated in London from Manchester for good political reasons, but it was from spinning sheds in towns like Nelson and Colne that their power was drawn. By 1896 five in every six working women belonged to cotton unions run almost exclusively by men. They didn't take much persuading to sign suffrage petitions, and the trainloads of women cotton-workers peacefully petitioning Westminster offered a calmer strategy to the middle-class guerrilla war waged by the Pankhursts.

Homo Northwestus at his best was a woman, binding together entire communities, and never letting the region down. Women like Bessie Braddock who battled for the poor in Parliament; MP for Liverpool Exchange for 25 years, attacking but never antagonising like some do today. She never dressed up like an Imelda Marcos either, and never had a personalised car number plate, but Bessie would get you a job or a council house and rumbustuously she gave voice to the North-West, and women, and the working-class movement.

It's the men who have shown our species up. Time after time Homo Northwestus has let loose some awful specimens who have baked hard the foreign myth of loud-mouthed, uncouth northern chauvinism. You can choose your own face to fit, anyone from an overweight comic to a shimmering-suited politician, and those old enough will conjure back the memory of Frank Randle, whose corner was the dirtiest of them all.

He was a comic, born in Wigan in 1901, and his act became one of the greatest, and smuttiest, music-hall turns of the 'thirties and 'forties. At fifteen he'd found work as a clown at a Blackpool circus, and later as the funny man in trapeze acts like the Three Ernestoes, the Bouncing Dillons or the Bouncing Randles. But he was as quick with his mouth as he was with his feet (and his fists), and his stage parodies of grotesque northern stereotypes quickly made him a hugely popular solo star.

But only in the North. There was something about the drunken, toothless geriatrics he created which held him here forever, fanatically adored at one thousand pounds a week in cash (on good nights), and abominated by the South. He was, according to the *Manchester Guardian*, the 'master of the single entendre,' and his coarse, direct earthiness appealed most to Homo Northwestus because here was a straight-talking species which had climbed out of the bog and could take it firmly on the chin.

Formby might be the golden boy, whose effortless transition into London's West End was bitterly resented by Randle, but it was

△ The Pankhursts; the strength of the suffragette movement was drawn from the Lancashire textile industry . . . even if the battle was won in London.

Frank who came closest to the fighting working-class heart of industrial Lancashire. His every mannerism and catchphrase – 'ah've supped some ale toneet' – mirrored a world of street-corner pubs and outside toilets that looked to Blackpool for its cultural Halvalla.

So when the morality squad of Blackpool constabulary weighed in against his 'grossly vulgar and suggestive' act in 1952, it was from the adoringly faithful jury of Central Pier Pavilion that Randle sought the only verdict that mattered.

'I come to you ladies and gentlemen and ask you to be my final judges. I am, like you, a simple man born of simple folk, a man of the industrial North of England. My pleasures are simple, my packet of Woodbines, my glass of Guinness, the simple joys of the seasons. Simple people of our kind understand the facts of life in a way that many of our critics do not . . . and because you understand life and the realities of life, I ask you to be my judges.'

'Tell 'em to get stuffed, Frank,' shouted one of the many cheering from the stalls.

But it didn't matter. Frank was slowly drowning in a sea of Scotch, surrounded by the flotsam of his increasingly violent moods. He'd take an axe to a dressing-room sink in a row over a drinks bill, shatter a mirror into a million pieces, shred a wardrobe into firewood. At a Barnsley theatre he ordered doors rehung because they squeaked, and his hotel bedrooms would run with splattered caviar.

> ❛ All over the North-West he had rocked the theatres with his drinking, farting, spewing string of innuendo. ❜

It wasn't all true, what they said, but contracts were cancelled and Randle faded, playing emptier houses and sometimes too drunk to summon together the familiar rubber contortions of his face. In the end it was gastro-enteritis which took him, on July 7th, 1957, sealing a grimly slow decline which had dragged Randle to the tearful bottom of his own immense personal despair.

Is this Homo Northwestus? In Blackpool on the piers, at the Accrington Hippodrome, all over the North-West, he had rocked the theatres with his drinking, farting, spewing string of innuendo. People here had taken to him as they took to George, but no two comics could have been further apart. Formby was village idiot; Randle, the school bully. But it was gormless George whose anodyne, innocent stupidity captured the hearts of all England,

FILM FUN

Frank Randle

Famous Star of Mancunian Films

1. Frank is called in to the television rehearsal to accompany Madam Screech on his accordion. "Delighted!" warbles he. "I will play accordion to instructions!"

2. But there's dirty work afoot. Buster Bank, the famous crook, has other fish to fry to-day and he finds Frank out of place. "A ball filled with ink will do the trick!" yaps he.

3. Sure enough, the next time Frank goes to squeeze his accordion he gets himself into a jam. "My character eet ees blackened!" howls Madam Screech. "'Ow dare you?"

4. "I daren't—and I didn't!" protests our pal. But the evidence is black against him. "Don't argue, chum," says the producer. "I wanted you to play the song, not the fool!"

5. "Never mind, Frank. Don't feel put out," says Stella, the studio lass. "Let's watch the rehearsal on this T.V. set." Frank agrees. "Screech will be a scream," says he.

6. When Madam Screech appears on the screen she is no longer black in the face, and her diamonds are so dazzling, Frank feels quite bright. But he's still in the dark!

7. "I've yet to find out who played that dirty trick on me," he tootles. "Hullo! What goes on here?" he adds. "Is this opera or drama? Someone's stopped Madam straining her tonsils and taken her diamonds!"

8. For a moment there is a blank blank on the screen. "Another technical 'itch'!" says Frank. "Why don't they come up to scratch!" Then Buster Bank appears, with the diamonds, and his hand is stained black!

9. "I'm ink-lined to think I'm on the trail of that trouble-maker!" warbles Frank. He stampedes into the studio with Stella. Everything's untidy, except the producer and Madam. They're so tied he hardly sees 'em.

10. Being a detective in his spare time, Frank doesn't have to dial 999 to find out who left the black hand-print on Madam Screech's dial. "His ink trick made me see red," chirps Frank, "but he's a marked man!"

11. "Oh, Frank!" coos Stella. "I really must hand it to you!" Frank modestly agrees he is the bright boy of the family. "This is quite a feat, catching a crook by hand!" he tootles. Then he calls the cops.

12. Buster Bank is severely arrested, and sentenced to be slapped on the left wrist with a wet kipper for snaffling Madam Screech's diamonds. As for Frank—he collects a special bonus, three hip-pips, and a hooray!

'A just passed a coupla tarts ont' rooid yonder. Eee, thi were a coupla hottunz. Hee . . . heee . . . but A took n'notice . . . much. A sed to 'er, A sed, "Not today, luv, A'd rayther 'ev a Kensitas" . . . Well, A woz 'eyvin' a bit o'fun wi' these youngunz. A took one o'em for a walk, about five mile. A sed, "A penny for yer thoughts" . . . Ooo she gimme such a clout across t'lug. A sed, "Wot's t'do wi'yi? I only sed a penny for yer thoughts." "Eee," she said, "A thowt yi sed a penny for mi shorts" . . .'

'Look at me. A'm 82. A could jump a five-bar gate . . . if it woz laid ont'floor like . . . It woz only t'other dee. A went to a funeral. A woz comin' awee from t'graveside. A chap looks at me, 'e sez, " 'Ow old are you?" A sed, "82." 'E sed, "A don't think it's much use you goin' 'ome at all" . . .'

Frank Randle's act, 1944.

⊲ The comics were good clean fun. The stage act of Randle wasn't.

and especially the South. Apart from the occasional song, no damage would be inflicted by this man's act. Here was no barbaric, threatening bog-man to remind us how divided the nation really was. Just as, later, Paul McCartney would be adopted by the public before acid-spitting John Lennon, so Formby flourished while Randle rankled. Homo Northwestus? He's schizophrenic.

Some blokes didn't let the side down. They were men who were the absolute opposite of Frank Randle; men who could be decent and gentle, and who heroically created the gentleman concept of Homo Northwestus. Sweet as a nut, they were; real cigarette-card heroes from a generation when footballers didn't charge a fee for a quote. It was the age of the gentleman-player, and from Lancashire you could fill a fleet of trams with their names. Today it's a news story when Gary Lineker gets through a season unbooked, but in Tom Finney's day it was the other way round. You didn't go sprawling for a penalty so often then and, anyway, players couldn't hear the ref for the clacking of massed, wooden rattles.

And when Nat Lofthouse turned out for Bolton Wanderers at Burnden Park, or Finney for Preston at Deepdale, they'd travel by bus or tram, mingling with the very spectators who paid their wages. 'I used to catch the corporation bus on the corner,' says Tom, 'and usually have quite a bit of fun talking with them about who you were going to play and the rough time you'd have . . . and on the way back if you had a bad game, or the team had a bad game, you did get some stick but you had a rapport with the supporters which is long ago gone.'

He'd pull on the Preston shirt through fourteen seasons and never once was Tom Finney booked. For his town he'd score 210 goals, for his country another thirty and, wherever he played in the 'forties and 'fifties, defenders and fans would be mesmerised by his skills. Nat Lofthouse, too, rarely troubled the referee, with just one booking, against Manchester City for throwing the ball at a linesman. Not that they were soft men; the game was harder then. 'I think if we had been playing in present conditions, I think you'd have had a job to finish the game,' says Nat. 'There would certainly have been a lot sent off the field for some of the offences they committed but in those days it was much more part and parcel of the game.'

In Bolton, up the Chorley New Road, there's a pub named after Nat Lofthouse – the Lion of Vienna – and although he no longer travels the tram on match days, he does still work in the town, as Finney does in Preston. Because, when their glory days were over, what some might see as temptation was not temptation

> ❜ Homo Northwestus had given the world its games and, thanks to an unknown Victorian, the time off to play them in. We'd invented the weekend! ❛

for them. They stayed, like Formby and Leverhulme, true to their species. Tom's a JP in Preston and still does the 'adding up' at the family plumbing business he started after the war with his brother. Nat's president of the Wanderers and a freeman of the borough he never deserted.

Says Tom, 'We were both local born and bred. We had our families and friends in and around Preston and Bolton and we never really had any wish to leave. I did have an offer to go to Italy in 1952 and was offered a ten thousand pound fee at a time when I was earning fourteen pounds a week as a professional player but I'd no inkling of wanting to move . . . and the club just wasn't interested.'

The North-West hadn't invented football – not quite – and there were great heroes at other clubs, but Conan Doyle was wrong again. When the Football League was established in 1888, five of the twelve founder members were clubs from cotton towns. Twenty-five years later every fourth club in the League was still a Lancashire team, and in other sporting pursuits Homo North-westus led the way. With Yorkshire's help he'd forged the Rugby League, and buried in a Manchester park was William Marsden, the pioneer of the Saturday half-day holiday. Homo Northwestus had given the world its games and, thanks to an unknown Victorian, the time off to play them in. We'd invented the weekend.

"TURF" CIGARETTES

TOM FINNEY
PRESTON N.E. & ENGLAND
50 FOOTBALLERS № 41

Benny Rothman took the time to go walking and, like thousands in the 'thirties, found he couldn't go where he wanted to go. Those saturated Pennine bogs which Homo Northwestus had abandoned centuries before now offered sanctuary for working people cramped in poor terraced housing, breathing foul, soot-dusty air. From dark, glowering towns they would flock to the fells to ramble where landowners said 'keep off' and gamekeepers upheld their law.

In 1932 Benny was twenty and on Kinder Scout there was not one single public footpath. By day he worked at Metro-Vicks on Trafford Park, but come evenings he was secretary of the Manchester-based British Workers Sports Federation, whose members were mostly his age and who all bitterly resented the privileged few who continued to deny moorland access to the underprivileged many. They planned a mass trespass and, on April 24th, six hundred walkers set off with two hundred Derbyshire policemen breathing heavily behind them. Although the press spoke of 'huge clashes', nothing too serious had happened that you could see. Benny made a speech; one policeman sprained an ankle; and by teatime five ramblers were locked up awaiting trial at New Mills and Derby.

△ The mass trespass on Kinder Scout in 1932. Thousands of working people found they couldn't walk free on the bogs they'd abandoned centuries before.

It was what you couldn't see that mattered at Kinder Scout. Benny, now a robust 81 years old, had elevated a local squabble into a national debate and, however slowly, the Pennine Moors would surely now be reopened. In 1949 the National Parks and Access to the Countryside Bill made it to the statute books, and the protection of Homo Northwestus's tribal homeland was, in part at least, assured. Through ordinary Joes like Benny Rothman, rambling had become a movement with a following of ordinary working people, free to step out for a blow on the bogs they had assumed were the inheritance of the species, not the lords and the landowners.

But then, Homo Northwestus always has been good at movements. He'd invented the Co-op in a Rochdale backstreet, and a stuttering abstainer in Preston had given the 't . . . t . . . tee . . . total' movement its otherwise inexplicable name. It was Lancashire where the world's first building society opened and, when it came to music, he was No. 1 from the Manchester sound and Wigan Soul to the Mersey Beat.

Although Homo Northwestus has generated no Shake-speare, no Anne Hathaway's cottage, he does have the beginnings of a rival to the tourist honeypots of those older, richer parts of merrie England. In three hundred years' time there will be no industry dedicated to any hero to match what Liverpool will do for The Beatles. Already there are chatty Beatle guides to escort you on two-hour trips around Penny Lane, Strawberry Fields, Lennon's home, McCartney's school, and what is curiously described as 'Ringoland'. There's a museum (open eight days a week) on the restored Albert Dock where you can buy a plaster replica of your favourite 'fab'. There are pubs. There are trinkets. There is the Merseyside Tourism Board which proclaims its ancient maritime port the 'City of the Beatles'. And all this while three of them still work, rest and play (although not necessarily in that order) far beyond the city which so hungrily markets them.

When the times changed, and rock and roll crashed through the previously melodious-sounding world, Homo Northwestus chose the key and played all the right notes. Just as Benny's boys shook an ancient landed order on Kinder Scout, so did the pop combos march out of basement clubs and milk bars to rattle and roll the grey suits of Wardour Street and London. Time and again, Homo Northwestus was the pick of the pops. The Swinging Blue Jeans. Wayne Fontana and the Mindbenders. Gerry and the Pacemakers. Freddie and the Dreamers. Billy J. Kramer. The Hollies. Cilla Black. Herman's Hermits. The Searchers.

On both sides of the Atlantic (for a time) it was Lancashire which set the style. So when Essex girls like Sandie Shaw sang barefooted, everyone knew it was a tame Carnaby Street clone of our Cilla, who could belt them out the best, as Gracie had some thirty years before. Lennon and McCartney (Irving Berlin and Noel Coward aside) had practically invented the pop song and went on to write all the best ones in the book, leaving only scraps for the two decades which followed them. But there was something else.

There was a belligerence, an heroic defiance in Lennon especially, that Homo Northwestus admired. While Randle stuck his V-sign at the South, Lennon lifted his middle finger at the world, and from that, via Alexei Sayle, a line can be drawn to the scallies and Happy Mondays of today; more caustic, more sussed than George Formby ever was. In the 'sixties Homo Northwestus had just the attitude, and Liverpool a double dose of it. In their

▽ Cilla Black . . . is she Maid Marion for Homo Northwestus?

I FREE POP TOKEN

films and from their heroes, people wanted young, civilised realism, having only scorn for the romantic reveries of balladeers and dialect poets.

It was Elsie Tanner and Albert Finney then. People with grit in their tonsils who had been bashed – like the tribe – but were fighting back in some terrible times. As mills went and docks closed, Homo Northwestus expected his heroes to take on the world and come home, like world champion boxer John Conteh, to the true Lancashire embrace. Like Manchester United with the European Cup, the biggest trophy tucked safely in their cupboard.

Do we have heroes any more, or just celebrities? Are we moved by a different spirit which is shallower, less altruistic, than that of past generations? And who chooses those we love? Derek Hatton was a hero in Liverpool, but perhaps not to so many now. George Best? Alex Higgins? Always, it seems, today's names are those footballers or sportsmen whose stature is measured by the weight of a pass, or the swerve of a cue ball.

There's a fair chance there'll be statues somewhere, some time, to Bobby Charlton and Paul McCartney. But Cilla Black and Owen Oyston? Probably not. James Anderton? Don't rule him out. And

The original Rochdale cowboy?

However unlikely it sounds, outlaw Butch Cassidy probably did speak with a Lancashire twang. His father, Maximilian Parker, was apparently one of many Preston Mormons who emigrated to the United States in the middle of the last century. He'd been born in 1844 and at the age of eleven he travelled to Utah where, in 1866, he fathered Robert Leroy Parker, the man the world now knows as Butch Cassidy.

Although Butch never left the States, he grew up in a tight Mormon community where the original accents of members were easily preserved. The Lancashire believers would have stayed together, and some stories claim that Butch liked to call his closest friends and associates 'chuck'.

How do we know? In the film, the Sundance Kid falls in love with Etta Place, whose real-life great-great-grandaughter now lives and works in the North-West of England. Whether or not Butch could claim to be the authentically-first Rochdale Cowboy is a matter of great historical debate . . .

Kenny Dalglish may yet appear in bronze in Blackburn, but definitely not in Liverpool, not now.

And these heroes send out what signals to the world? That Homo Northwestus is warm-hearted and honest like Tom Finney and Nat Lofthouse? Or smart and independent like Gracie? That we are tough, belligerent and defiant like Lennon and Randle . . . or Butch Cassidy? Who, if anyone, encapsulates all these qualities and whose statue should be in every park in every town in the North-West?

There is one nominee. Someone who was self-made and stayed in the region. Someone who stayed the course – winning, often as not – but who was graceful in defeat. Someone who tried hard not to sit on the fence, who liked a drink, and who once even switched on the Blackpool illuminations.

Red Rum. Who else?

▽ The North-West's most unimpeachable hero? Fifteen years after his last Grand National there are politicians who would kill for Red Rum's popularity ratings.

Chapter FIVE

The panda's tale

ON a hill rising out of the steep, narrow streets of Lancaster looms the dark outline of an unmistakable Lancashire landmark: the castle. If you go through the black-studded oak of John of Gaunt's front door you'll be welcomed by men in peaked hats. These are prison officers and this is one of the oldest working prisons in the world.

Between the twin turrets of its gateway have passed all manner of offenders from the heinous to the petty to the mad. The castle's cells have held witches, martyrs and lunatics. Some went in never to come out. Some went in to be tried and found guilty, like the Birmingham Six, only to come out from other jails as innocent men years later. And today, after nine hundred years, it's facing a future where people actually pay to go in. The prison is due to close, its inmates rehoused, and a new destiny devised for this oldest of buildings. A hotel, maybe, or a theme park. In the end it may be the Queen herself who decides.

The castle site is as old as Lancashire itself. A prime site perched above the Lune, it was chosen by the Norman, Roger of Poitou, as the place from which to run the land given to him by his jubilant boss, William the Conqueror. As bit was added to bit the shape of modern Lancashire was slowly defined, making Roger of Poitou – who spoke French – the first consciously North-Western *Homo Northwestus* on historical record. It's ironic that it was a foreigner who moulded a boundary that would, in large part, survive until 1974 when local government re-organisation dismantled its old,

> 6 Between the twin turrets of its gateway have passed all manner of offenders, from the heinous to the petty to the mad. 9

sentimental logic.

He'd chosen a good spot, had Roger. From the castle keep, then wooden, he could command the crucial intersection of key, strategic routes. Up the Lune Valley ran the main trans-Pennine track to Yorkshire. The A6, as it now is, funnelled north on the eastern fringe of his new headquarters. And across the sands of Morecambe Bay, when the tide was low, a connection could be made to the crucial communities of South Cumbria, where the first of the species had hunted elk centuries before.

For three centuries after Roger, the castle changed hands more often than the FA Cup until, in 1361, it fell into the hands of John of Gaunt, the first Duke of Lancaster and one of the richest men in medieval England – £12,000 a year which, at today's seasonally adjusted figures, would be bringing him a staggering £25 million. No wonder he stayed faithful to the King, Richard II. No wonder his son Henry was fed up when Richard banished him and pinched his lands after John of Gaunt died. No wonder Henry came back – showing true Homo Northwestus grit – to claim his Duchy and the Crown, thereby establishing the inseparable link between the Crown and the Red Rose county which exists today. Look on the side of Lancaster Castle. There's a sign which tells you who owns it. It's the Queen.

△ An unmistakable Lancashire landmark, the gatehouse of Lancaster Castle.

Lancashire is proud of that tradition. It's proud of others, too, and that's why, on a wet summer's morning, a procession will wend from Lancaster's historic priory to the castle, looking appropriately antique and dignified and serious. It will be led by the Under-Sheriff of the county and will include a brace of judges, a delegate from the Chief Constable, the Norroy and Ulster King of Arms and the newly-appointed High Sheriff of Lancashire. Some of them look as if they've stepped out of a pack of cards. Hard on their heels will come the mayoral party and after them, clutching their hats (for it is raining steadily now), the ladies, who have come to see their men conduct themselves with dignity and decorum.

Despite the blistering rain of June, a fanfare of trumpets will be blasted by the county police as the procession moves, with all available pomp and circumstance, towards what could be mistaken for the tradesmen's entrance of the castle. But though this slow procession has an aura of timelessness, it's all a bit of a *trompe l'oeil* for, in reality, it's a more recent re-creation of a Lancashire never-never land that never ever was.

This is the Hanging of the Shield, an annual ceremony with a ritual all of its own. After a service at the Priory Church of St. Mary, redolent with choir boys and the old familiar hymns, the participants make for the back door of the castle and enter – not to the nick, but to the grand Shire Hall. Here the new High Sheriff will ask the Constable of the castle to receive his shield. The Norroy and Ulster King of Arms (the Chief Herald in those parts of the kingdom lying north of the Trent) will step forward briskly to approve its heraldic correctness and the Constable of the Castle will hang the new shield on the wall between the last Constable's and his own. A rapid signature, a quick photo-call, and the chief protagonists are away. The shield-hanging doesn't quite last long enough really to gather momentum.

This year the new High Sheriff was John Holt; his new motto 'Know Thyself'; his new coat of arms (given the nod by the Norroy and Ulster Kings of Arms) created specially for the occasion. It depicts three otters; for the College of Arms likes nothing better than a pun and it is otters, of course, who live in a holt. The office of High Sheriff is mainly ceremonial now; for his year of office John Holt will effectively become a county-wide mayor, looking after High Court Judges when they are in the neighbourhood and generally acknowledging the good works of others. It is his Under-Sheriff, Andrew Wilson, who works at the sharp end of the system, enforcing High Court writs throughout the county as his family has been doing for the last 150 years.

> 6 This species of "pandas" lives between motorways, in leafy habitats where it seems as if the 20th century had not yet arrived. 9

John's is the 569th shield to hang in the Shire Hall – they vary from the distinguished to the droll. Amongst the creatures rampant and couchant you'll find Mr. Fordyce of Feniscowles' Four Dice, and Mr. Greenwood of Whalley's red, crossed Whales. You will also see fistfuls of other names: Pilkingtons; Stanleys; Towneleys; and Blundells; respectable old Lancashire names that echo down through the centuries from the 1300s to today.

In a county of immigrants where so many of us are new, just a few of the old families have survived. They are only a tiny proportion of Homo Northwestus: a rare breed; an honourable, endangered species who have carefully kept their heads in the troubled days when, all around, others were losing theirs. This species of our very own, these pandas, live between the motorways in leafy habitats where it sometimes seems as though that other Lancashire of Frank Randle, of Joe Bloggs and the Beatles, had never happened; where it almost seems as if the twentieth century had not yet arrived.

Mark Blundell is one of them. His home, Crosby Hall, is a modest stately home, still substantial, though greatly reduced in size through economic circumstance. It is an improbable rural idyll, approached by a crunchy gravel drive, grazed about by Constable-ish cattle, a world away from Liverpool – a city living and dying and trying to rise again just beyond the estate boundary wall. Mark's family moved to Little Crosby in 1362 and they've been there ever since – 22 generations on the same spot. Because of that you can't escape the feeling that, while cities come and go, the Blundells will go on forever. 'Liverpool's a little fledgling, really, compared with the people who live around here,' comments Mark. 'Not just the Blundells, but many other families in the village go back probably as long as we do.'

Mark Blundell is a gentle gentleman, married to a Swiss wife and the father of two daughters. He is informal, greeting us in an open-necked shirt, with a bike leaning carelessly against a bannister in the hall; but his book-lined, soft-lit library argues a long family history of substance and culture. He is self-deprecating about his family's achievements: 'The Blundells haven't done very much – they've just been here a very long time'. What the family has been, and what Mark plays down, is staunchly committed to Catholicism, through thick and thin, in common with several of the other landed families of Lancashire.

Much of the county chose to ignore the Reformation and, by the middle of Elizabeth I's reign, Lancashire was already recognized as being the most Catholic county in England. In 1581 fines for non-attendance at church were £20 a month and for hearing Mass the penalties included imprisonment and swingeing fines. But nothing could stamp out the old religion. The tribe was stubborn; it was in its nature. In 1640 only 2% of the national population was Catholic

△ Armorial bearings like that of the Blundells of Little Crosby were once the universally recognised badges of the gentry.

– but in Lancashire it was 20%. During the seventeenth and eighteenth centuries it was reckoned that a quarter of all the Catholics in England and Wales lived here.

The Catholic community differed in its visibility; there were the out-and-out refuseniks – the recusants – who would not attend Anglican church services; there were the church papists, who attended Anglican services, but in body alone – they declined the Anglican communion; and there were the Anglican stalwarts who kept their old religion more discreetly, but who were unlikely to shop their higher-profile Catholic neighbours. In such an atmosphere, though penal legislation looked very grim on paper it proved, in Lancashire, to be very difficult to enforce.

That's not to say that Catholicism wasn't a risky business. There were Catholic martyrs; men like Lawrence Johnson from Great Crosby, a missionary priest arrested in 1581 and hanged, drawn and quartered at Tyburn the following year; Richard Hurst, a farmer, taken in his fields near Broughton in the Fylde and hanged at Lancaster on 29th August 1628; and Edmund Arrowsmith, a Jesuit missionary from Warrington and 'a persuader in religion', hanged, drawn and quartered at Lancaster on 28th August 1628. And there were others.

> ❛ Many of Lancashire's landed gentry families succumbed to the financial temptation to sell ancestral homes and abandon the North-West. ❜

The Blundells ran the gauntlet of anti-Catholic persecution. In 1590 Richard Blundell and his son William were seized by Lord Derby, the Lord Lieutenant, together with Robert Woodruffe, a Catholic priest who was in hiding at Crosby Hall. The Blundells ended up in Lancaster Castle, Richard succumbing to gaol fever from which he died the following year.

William, known as 'the Recusant', spent a further three years in prison, was released in 1595 and outlawed again in 1599. On the accession of James I he was allowed to return to Little Crosby, but subsequently two thirds of his estate was seized for non-payment of recusancy fines.

But the nineteenth century was kinder to the Blundells. For so long on the wrong side of the financial tracks they were, after Catholic Emancipation, able to make a killing out of Liverpool's success. 'When the industrial revolution came, what were the benefits?' Ray asked Mark.

'There were financial benefits definitely in the nineteenth

century when Liverpool became one of the richest cities in the world. The Blundells were able to take advantage of that by selling land for housing, notably Blundell Sands, which was turned into desirable commuter residences for the merchants and professional classes of the city of Liverpool.'

Industrialisation was a double-edged sword for the North-Western landed gentry. The pressures of urbanisation squeezed out the country estate and, though they were tempted to make a packet through selling up, they knew they would lose their old ancestral homes. But enough did succumb to the ready money, and the result has been a dearth of old money and a dearth of old houses, especially in the south of the region.

On the human scale it meant a dearth, too, of a landed gentry peer group, and from the sanctuary of Crosby Hall, Mark Blundell will admit that the North-West can feel isolated. There is much more of a landed family social scene in the South of England.

But Mark Blundell is Homo Northwestus and he's here to stay. Those that survived were tough and, true to Blundell type, he is not going to be frightened out, bought out or frozen out. Though there might be a momentary sense of relief if he were forced to leave, his overriding feeling would be one of sadness at having to abandon something which has gone on for so long. He is convinced that families such as his own have a future: 'Several hundreds of years ago, the landed families had an important part to play in the sense that they were the social focus and the political and economic focus of a lot of the activity of the region. I think that became less important in the nineteenth century when they became perhaps less involved in local affairs and lived much more for themselves – in their own social sphere. I feel that's changing again now, and I feel the justification for the survival of the old families will be if they can become more involved, more integrated into the communities to which they belong.'

Despite the labradors and the public school inflection, Mark Blundell is a thoroughly modern landowner with a social conscience – the gentry's answer to Prince Charles. When he came back to Crosby Hall after having lived for ten years in London, he found it rather strange to be sitting in 120 acres of his own parkland on the edge of a very urban area. He has responded by opening the doors of his estate; not to coachloads of paying visitors, whom he feels would swamp his home, but to classrooms-full of cheerful nine year olds who come to take advantage of the Crosby

△ Simon Towneley – the Queen's man in Lancashire.

countryside. Now in these quieter days the only hunting done at Crosby Hall is scavenger hunting and the only invigilation is of birds and bats.

On the other side of the old county, at Dyneley, close by ivy-clad Towneley Hall near Burnley, lives Simon Towneley, who now rather regrets the loss of Towneley Hall – his family's seat from the fourteenth century to 1902. At the end of the last century, he told us sadly, the Towneley acres were divided between six co-heiresses and the Hall subsequently municipalised and sold to Burnley Corporation for £17,500. It is a museum and art gallery now and much visited by locals, but you feel Simon would still like to promenade by the lily pond or throw the occasional party in Towneley's lofty baroque Hall. Though he may not manage the latter, he still does attend a family mass once a year at All Hallows Eve in the tiny oak chapel. Simon is dapper, rosy, witty, the writer of *Venetian Opera in the Seventeenth Century*; a Fellow of the Royal Northern College of Music; a director of Granada Television; some-time Colonel-in-Chief of the Duke of Lancaster's Own

Yeomanry; some-time Chairman of the Northern Ballet Theatre. He is also a gentleman landowner and the first Catholic Lord Lieutenant of the County since the Reformation.

As with so many of the species, Homo Northwestus, Simon is a mix. His father was a Belgian colonel in the Irish Guards, and the Towneley name and property has come down from his mother's side.

Like the Blundells, his family kept alight the Catholic flame locally but they suffered for their faith, undergoing imprisonment and the sequestration of their estates. For 260 years they were effectively excluded from public affairs in which they had formerly been prominent. Simon Towneley can see, though, that there were certain advantages in his family's having gone to ground. 'If they had been Protestants I suppose they would have gone to court or to London, made a lot of money, perhaps . . . and *spent* a lot of money.'

> **❛ In a fittingly Lancastrian piece of research, it was Towneley where rainfall was first measured. ❜**

But, unseduced by the distraction of the metropolis, the family concentrated its energies elsewhere. In a fittingly Lancastrian piece of research, it was Towneley Hall where rainfall was first measured, outside the bedroom window of Richard Towneley in the years between 1677 and 1703. Richard was also a noted philosopher and mathematician, involved in the formation of Boyle's Law and a friend of the Astronomer Royal, John Flamsteed. Together they first accurately charted the movements of Jupiter. But Simon's soulmate was Charles Towneley, Charles the Connoisseur who, in the late eighteenth century, made the famous collection of classical sculpture which is now kept in the British Museum.

Simon's favourite family story, though, is of Francis Towneley, who threw in his lot with the Young Pretender; Francis was colonel of the Manchester Regiment and was captured, allegedly playing the mouth organ, at Carlisle on the rebel retreat to Scotland. What happened to him next has become something of a well-honed family tale: 'He was condemned for treason and executed and his head was put on Temple Bar, which I think is the normal practice. But it found its way back to Towneley, where it was kept in the chapel and I think it was embalmed and so it was fairly well-preserved. Then, when central heating was put in the house at the end of the last century, the pipes went behind the panelling and cooked the head, really, and all the flesh fell off – and it was then

△ Flash photography . . . an unusual view of Towneley Hall.

put in a hat box, where it used to be handed round after dinner when there was a lot of port being drunk.'

With Catholic emancipation in 1828 the family came out of purdah and resumed their position in society. Simon's great great grandfather, Peregrine, was appointed High Sheriff of Lancashire, a position which Simon himself held in 1971. Now he is Lord Lieutenant of Lancashire, has been since 1976, hosting the Royal Family when they are in the county and upholding the dignity of the Crown when they are not. He enjoys his position: 'One of the joys of being a Lord Lieutenant is that one does move around rather like the joker in the pack,' he says with a chuckle.

Simon believes in the value and influence of old families. They've been around so long that he regards them as a kind of social ballast: 'I think there is still a certain amount of influence, maybe because if you own land, you are less likely to move away, less likely to pack up and move house. So in that sense you are always there and people tend to consult you about things simply as a sort of lodestar – a sort of stable part of the community.'

Mark Blundell and Simon Towneley may be old money and old families, but the greatest Homo Northwestus of us all is certainly not a Catholic. She wasn't even born in the county, and she doesn't even have a home here. She is the Queen – the Duke of Lancaster – and always referred to as such when glasses are clinked in the loyal toast throughout the county. It is said to be, of the Queen's many titles, her favourite.

> **The Duke of Lancaster isn't a Catholic; she wasn't born in the county and doesn't even have a home here: she is the Queen.**

After Henry Bolingbroke returned from exile to retrieve his rightful inheritance he decreed that his Duchy should remain an entity distinct from the Crown, a separate family inheritance. And so it is still, six hundred years later. But while the Duchy used to be a huge landholding with property in every corner of England, over the centuries much of it was sold off to pay for the King's wars. By the late seventeenth century it was on the verge of bankruptcy, the rot eventually being stopped by Queen Anne, and *The Independent* claimed last year that the Duchy now yields the Queen over £3 million a year, tax free. For the time being.

Today it is Mr. Parsons who is the Duchy's surveyor of lands and runs the Duchy office at Forton, outside Lancaster. Up here, the

Duchy's main lands are now in Lancashire, South Cheshire and Yorkshire, each running to about twelve thousand acres, together with other scattered holdings in the South of England. In Lancashire itself the Duchy owns five estates – 45 farms in all: Winmarleigh Moss (for its shooting rights); Dolphinholme (where they've newly diversified into a fishery and you can rent a chalet for the week); Myerscough in the Fylde; Salwick near Preston; and Whitewell in the Hodder Valley. Only Myerscough has been traditionally Duchy land; the other properties were acquired this century – Whitewell from the Towneleys. The Duchy also owns most of the Lancashire foreshore, that area of land between high and low water mark. The bits that were of commercial value were sold off long ago to bodies like Blackpool Council and the Mersey Docks and Harbour Board, and now they have over 100,000 hectares of no real use to anyone except for wading birds and wildfowl – like the Ribble up to Preston, the Duddon estuary and the tide-washed sands of Morecambe Bay, where Jack Manning from Flookburgh finds his shrimps and over which the Duchy still appoints sand-pilot to guide travellers across the perilous sand flats.

△   Flookburgh fisherman, Jack Manning.

Mr. and Mrs. Proctor Hall are tenants of the Queen who live at a farmhouse at Dolphinholme, festooned with hanging baskets, and looking for all the world like Cotswold stone, though it's really millstone grit. The farmhouse is about a hundred yards from the River Wyre – peaty brown and trout-filled at this point – and is dominated by a huge and rusty millwheel.

The Halls are proud to be Duchy tenants: 'Not everyone can have a Duchy farm, and if someone asks you who your landlord is, it's nice to be able to say, "The Queen" '. They have met the Duke of Lancaster three times now. Once formally on a local official visit; the second time at Whitewell when the pheasants got in the flower arrangement and 'she wasn't the Queen, she was just the Landlord' (though not, presumably, your average Lancashire landlady); and the third time at the Palace itself.

The Duchy does its tenants proud when they go down to the Palace; seats are booked for them on the train and lunch laid on at The Savoy. 'I think the Duchy means a lot to her,' says Mrs. Hall. 'When you go to the Palace, the Duchy tenants are always the first to meet her. The royal party make a beeline for you. They chat about the area. They're up here more often than you think. The Duke looked at our feet and said, "I'm surprised they're not webbed because it is always raining when I go up there" '.

I f the Queen is the Duke of Lancaster, the Derbys were its Kings. In seemingly every town in Lancashire a street corner will bear their name (Stanley Street), or a pub their family crest (The Eagle and Child). They permeate the county. The present Lord Derby, the eighteenth in the series, still lives at Knowsley, though not now in the great house of his ancestors, into which his

▷ Edward John Stanley, the 18th Earl of Derby. Making a point to Ray in the grounds of his Knowsley Park home.

◁ Amazingly, there are no reliable pictures of the first Lathom House, the one that Lady Derby defended so stoutly for the King during the Civil War. This engraving shows its scale, though.

family moved after the Civil War. Lord Derby's new ducal residence looks austere from the outside, its contours still unsoftened by age and weather. Inside it feels, momentarily, like a lateral version of *Upstairs Downstairs* – Lord Derby and his dogs at the front of the house and his lively, lippy, Scouse retainers at the rear. But his study, where he relaxes us, is not that of a severe man; there are towels on the armchairs for his dogs and 'Swoop' on the windowsill for the wild birds. It is to his window that the pheasants come for sanctuary when they hear the guns.

His earldom was created in 1485. Till then the Derbys were plain Stanleys, but at Bosworth Field they showed a well-developed knack for backing the winning side. The eighteenth Earl rather approves: 'I admired the first one. He was incredibly clever. As you know, the Wars of the Roses lasted a long time, and first one side was in power and then the other, and he very successfully engineered his life so that he was always in with the one who was in power'. Whenever Thomas Stanley was required to raise an army, he would duly raise it but ensure that it never arrived on the scene early enough to get embroiled in the fighting. True to form, at Bosworth, Thomas lingered long enough to calculate who was going to come out top dog and, at the last minute, committed his troops to an attack on Richard's hard-pressed troops just before they scattered and fled. Thomas then had the admirable nerve to claim his intervention had been the decisive factor in Henry of Richmond's victory.

Whether for his cheek or for his loyalty, he was rewarded with the Earldom of Derby, conferred upon him three days before Henry was crowned Henry VII, together with valuable lands which had belonged to the Harrington and Pilkington families.

> **6 There was scarcely a corner of Lancashire in which the Derby family did not wield power. 9**

The family's relationship with Lancashire was unique. There was scarcely a corner of Lancashire in which the Derby family did not wield power and influence. It was a relationship consolidated politically in the sixteenth century when the third Earl was granted governmental powers within the county. From now on the Crown would rule Lancashire through the Derbys. Homo Northwestus, ruled by proxy.

The third Earl would seem to have savoured his position to the full. He kept a household of over a hundred retainers, a high number even in 1561, and in that year had to meet bills for £1500 for food, £81 for wine (still a luxury in Lancashire) and £131 for fruit and spices. He steered a careful course through the religious minefield of the Elizabethan reign, arraigning, amongst others, John Towneley for non-compliance with the new religious laws, but showing too much sympathy with the recusant position to deal harshly with him. It was his son, however, the fourth Earl, who called on Richard and William Blundell in 1590 and despatched them to Lancaster prison.

Today's eighteenth Earl has other family favourites: the twelfth Earl, the founder of the Oaks and the Derby, and the thirteenth Earl who kept a menagerie at Knowsley which is said to have cost him £10,000 a year. There were zebras, antelopes, eland, gazelle, yaks and gnus and kangaroos. It was the thirteenth Earl who brought Edward Lear, then an ornithological draughtsman, to Knowsley to record his collection, and it was at Knowsley that Lear wrote the nonsense verses for the Derby children. It seems appropriate that, six generations later, the eighteenth Earl has created a new menagerie at Knowsley – his favourites not the eye-catching carnivores or mega-mammals but rather the most natural and ordinary of animals – the black buck and fallow deer.

But it is Lord Derby's grandfather whom he recalls with the

greatest warmth: 'I had a tremendous affection for my grandfather, he was a wonderful grandfather, quite apart from being a very remarkable man'. The seventeenth Earl, whom Lord Derby succeeded, for his grandfather lived to be a very old man and his father didn't, was a larger-than-life figure, a truly giant panda: an MP in 1892; Director of Recruiting in 1915; Secretary of State for War from 1916 to 1918; Ambassador Extraordinary to France 1918 to 1920; Chairman of the Liverpool Chamber of Commerce for 32 years; President of the British Cotton Growing Association for 25 years; Winner of the Derby, the St. Leger and the Oaks; Lord Mayor of Liverpool; a hero of the Turf, King of Lancashire. 'The last of the grand seigneurs,' says his grandson, sadly. 'For instance, on his seventieth birthday some 70,000 people subscribed to his birthday present – people from all walks of life – in fact there are twelve volumes of their signatures in the big house. I can't think of anybody else in our lifetime who, on their seventieth birthday,' added the 74 year old Duke, 'has been acknowledged by the people of their county. I can't think of anyone in the country who had that sort of relationship with the county.'

Of course it is different now, and the Kings of Lancashire are ghosts. 'Do you think the relationship has changed between your family and Lancashire?' Ray asked Lord Derby.

'Well, life has changed, hasn't it? You couldn't expect it to happen today. We live in a very different changing world . . . It's the politicians who have the power and influence today.'

The eighteenth Earl is no slouch: he had a distinguished military career, abbreviated by the need to take over his family responsibilities; he was Lord Lieutenant of the county for seventeen years; he is President of the Rugby Football League; a keen racehorse owner and still the Constable of the Castle at Lancaster – it was he who hung John Holt's new shield on the wall of the Shire Hall – but it must be hard not to feel overshadowed by such a dynasty of over-achievers and he says he finds it difficult to see how in comparison with the past, old families can make a very big contribution or have a big effect today.

The old house proved a burden and Lord Derby and his late wife pulled huge parts of it down – 66 rooms – but still found it uninhabitable. Now one wing is used by the police and the rest remains curiously frozen in time. The family portraits are still there, from the first Earl to himself, thickly hung in the chilly state dining room and wrought by the hands of the foremost painters of the day: Gainsborough, Ghaerhardt, Lely, Kneller. But Lord Derby has decamped to his more modest accommodation, to a house you can call a home, though still on the estate, for he will never leave Knowsley – better known now for its Safari Park than for being the power-house of power brokers.

None of our old families has retained its entire ancestral holdings or its ancestral grip on power. Many of them and many of the new millocracy moved out of Lancashire with their money to go where the hunting, shooting and fishing were better, or to new county estates nearer the metropolis. Other families simply became extinct; their palaces now over-built or ruined.

In the early eighteenth century, after the Derbys had left their former seat of Lathom for Knowsley, Sir Thomas Bootle, the Prince of Wales's Chancellor, built there a Palladian palace, designed by Giacomo Leoni. His niece inherited the estate and her grandson was made the first Earl of Lathom – but two generations later and it was all over. The third Earl blew the family fortunes. Homo Northwestus Gatsby. A friend and patron of Noel Coward, he spent most of his life abroad. A long-time bachelor, he married three years before his death, but by then he was not sufficiently creditworthy for the Ritz to trust his cheques, and they asked for payment in advance for his reception.

Lathom House was plundered, pulled down in 1925, and the estate sold off to pay Lathom's debts. Now only the faintest echoes are left along with the old stable block, falling stone by stone into oblivion.

> ‘ The writer Evelyn Waugh described the Cliftons as “tearing mad”. ’

Another burnt-out branch of the panda species are the Cliftons, originally of Salwick and later of Lytham, an old Lancashire line whose descendants Evelyn Waugh was later to describe as ‘tearing mad’. Harry, their last giant panda, squandered £3½ million in the last, sad days of this great South Fylde estate.

The Cliftons were a major Catholic family whose members included MPs, High Sheriffs and soldiers who fought at Agincourt. Like many of the recusant families, the Cliftons hid Catholic priests, and it is said, too, that they kept at Lytham the clothes of the martyred Jesuit, Edmund Arrowsmith, and the knife with which his body had been mutilated after his execution at Lancaster.

Clifton Hall, their airy and elegant Georgian mansion of red brick, survives. It was built by John Carr of York for Thomas Clifton between 1757 and 1764. Its ceilings are elaborately plastered, the most striking being the one above the handsome staircase, which depicts Jupiter hurling down thunderbolts from heaven. When you hear of their later family history you can almost understand his exasperation.

The Cliftons seem to have felt beset by the new Lancashire, by rough-hewn Homo Northwestus, and out-numbered. Thomas Clifton complained in 1848, 'I must confess to some prejudice against the class to which Mr. Hornby belongs. Cotton spinners and persons who have the constant habit of driving bargains are always attempting to overreach themselves'. Twenty years afterwards Lady Clifton felt an equal distaste: 'We have the misfortune to belong to a county where merchants and wealth are far above, in their own opinion, the aristocracy and the old landed gentry'.

The Clifton response was flight. John Talbot Clifton largely abandoned Lytham for Northamptonshire, London and the Mediterranean and his grandson, another John Talbot, went even further. For years he led a reckless and wandering life – living alone with the eskimos, hunting musk ox in Hudson Bay, attempting to become a correspondent in the Boer War, finding a wife in Peru and spending money throughout his excursions as if there were no tomorrow. He finally settled down to be Squire of Lytham in 1907 at the age of 39. On his death, a friend wrote of him: 'Of what use were all his expensive and spasmodic excursions? What did he achieve? Nothing. Nothing in the huckster's view or the view of the solicitor's clerk. He was noble, aimless, irascible, bullying, dauntless, extravagant, generous, scorning craftiness or thrift, golden-hearted, golden-fisted, fast to his friend – a figure unhorsed into our humdrum days from Roncesvalles or Fontarrabia'.

But it was Harry who finally ended the family's long relationship with Lytham. Harry out-Randled Frank, selling off his lands piecemeal to pay for planes and racehorses, for Gaugins and Tissots and gold Fabergé eggs. In Los Angeles he played poker with Lew Brice and, in a single game, lost $340,000.

John Kennedy was Harry's land agent at Lytham, and he has written about him in *The Clifton Chronicle*. He tells how boxes would arrive at Lytham from Harry's travels, full of tortoises; four tons of Indian gods turned up at Lytham goods station, but when Harry died in 1976 there was only £30,000 left in the pot, which he bequeathed to a Blackpool fortune-teller who, it is said, was last heard of telling the fortunes of dogs in America.

The cleaners will tell you that the Cliftons are still there, at least in spirit, they pass them with a whiff of perfume and impishly switch on and off their hoovers; but, physically at least, the hall is now owned by the Guardian Royal Exchange.

So many of our pandas are extinct, escaped, or were shouldered out by new industrial brass; their fortunes blown up or spent abroad. And now it seems as if more ordinary Northwesti can step into their empty shoes to fill the functions the Duchy requires.

Lancashire's new High Sheriff, John Holt, is not a panda. He's one of us, a working farmer looking after his own patch in the Lune Valley and employing five people. His family were from Bury, millowners from deep industrial Lancashire, but they sold up and moved here and in the fullness of time John became a farmer and married the girl next door, whose own family had roots in dirty Oldham coal. John played his Lancashire part; stood for the council; did charitable work; and so, in time, those mysterious ones whose job it is to spot our new High Sheriffs looked him over for the job, checked him out, and gave his name to the Queen.

The pandas of Lancashire, more than those of any other county, took a pounding in the last two hundred years. Into their ancient homes now goes new money and no-one can be sure in the next two hundred years where the new money will come from. Theoretically the Duke of Lancaster, the Queen, could choose any one of the tribe as the ceremonial head of the species, the High Sheriff of Lancashire. Perhaps, in the future, she will.

The Abergele Retired Gentlemen's Club meets every other Thursday in a soporifically warm converted schoolhouse opposite the town's main garage. Resplendent in casual beige jackets or blazers, they'll arrive shortly after lunch, just as the Abergele Welsh language group go into session in the room next to theirs.

Not that the clash will present many retired gents with a dilemma. Apart from one who is learning the native tongue, these are exiles; not from Wales, but living in Wales, as voluntary refugees from a Lancashire they now mostly despair of. 'Dreadful' is an adjective they will commonly apply to their old turf, and not one is unhappy with the biting surf or the rattling sea of his adopted and adored Abergele.

The *Liverpool Echo* and the *Manchester Evening News* may sell well in local newsagents, but they are read and passed around for their hard news, not out of any sense of regret. In the Abergele Retired Gentlemen's Club everyone speaks with the same voice. Coming to North Wales was the best decision of their lives.

When the Abergele gents pack their bags for their annual trip this year they'll be forsaking the rheumatic winds of the North for the milder air of Bournemouth. It should be noted, however, that few of them will be lured to stay by the kinder climate.

In Abergele it's the kindness of the people that counts and by all accounts there's more of that than the beach has pebbles. Take

chairman Bill Perrins, for example. For 23 years he worked in Essex where his sanity was preserved by his marriage to a Manchester woman.

'In Essex,' says Bill, 'you can walk down the street and no-one will give you a second glance. But up here the Welsh people, and the retired people, will happily join you on a park bench for a chat . . . there's no need to be lonely in Abergele.'

Bill retired to North Wales six years ago and likes to think of the Abergele Retired Gentlemen as a 'friendship club', an organisation providing company and help: 'We had the floods and one member lost everything in his garden, so we could give him a cheque for £50 to start him up again.'

They also have four sick visitors who ensure a get-well card is sent whenever a member falls ill, and if someone dies they're on hand with 160 pairs of shoulders to cry on. 'When you've retired there might not be many people around to go to the funeral of a loved one . . . but when 20 or 30 of the lads arrive we can really cheer people up.'

<table>
<tr><td>Chapter
SIX</td><td># Roll over George Formby</td></tr>
</table>

A T the masked charity ball in Cheshire's Lord Daresbury Hotel, everyone was of one mind; choosing the best male mask was a doddle. Rising from the sharp fold of the winner's shirt collar was a sun-swamped desert island scene painted directly onto his skin like some ghastly technicolour tattoo. In front of his left ear a skinny palm tree had taken root on pale yellow sand. His forehead had been transformed into a thin blue Caribbean sky and for all the world he looked like a walking travel brochure. Perhaps it was slightly intimidating (a bit like some up-market skinhead), but nothing else among the bobbing, glittering disguises on sticks came within an inch for class. Not the bird-like beak masks, or the lamé Lone Ranger lookalikes with their coiffured peacock quills and elaborate, rustling tassels.

They'd come, these 160 party people, to raise money for charity. In their shivering frocks and dinner suits, they'd found their places at tables for ten which they, or some corporate host, had paid £300 for. There were flowers for the ladies at the door and, although Glenda Jackson could not be there (as first hoped), Lord, formerly Len, Murray was on hand to make a suitable, if subdued substitute. Eileen Bilton was there, too, tall and slim in full-length incandescent black, enjoying the fruits of her own mission to raise £100,000 for the National Children's Home Warrington appeal.

Beyond midnight they danced to the music of the Cavaliers – 'sixties a speciality – until in a sea of shredded balloons, the ball was over with not a pumpkin in sight . . .

It's over, finished and popped. That old idea people had of Lancashire has gone. Although, once, masked balls might have been the preserve of deepest, snootiest Cheshire, now you can find them, and the people who might go to them, practically anywhere. Eileen Bilton's evening unfolded just a handful of miles south of Warrington. Warrington? Fifteen years ago it was busy but blighted, and now it's thriving and rising under new management; not in old Lancashire, but new Cheshire. No wonder Eileen Bilton's smile is so wide between her twin columns of straight, jet hair. To many it was her name – ring Eileen Bilton – that put an entire community back on the map. Single-handed, some say in jest, she's rebuilt the North-West and now everyone wants a chunk of it. Homo Northwestus is a match for Homo Home Counties any day of the week. Look at the facts. Look at the Football League.

How many people under forty have ever worked inside a cotton mill? How many under fifty? The mills are silent, converted into laundromats or carpet warehouses, and people seep out of the towns for the good, clean life in the suburbs. Wilmslow, Hale, Altrincham, Neston. And it's not just happening in Cheshire, but in ever-posher Lancashire too, with second homes (for the few) in all sorts of places. Ever more this is normal life, not just for giant pandas, and Homo Northwestus loves it. The smog is gone. The grime is gone. The slums are going (or changing). L. S. Lowry is dead. Roll over George Formby.

But the purpose of this final chapter is to ask what comes into the vacuum to replace those special qualities – of work, and warm-hearted backstreets – that truly did bind Homo Northwestus together, make him almost a species apart? What is the tribe becoming? What remains to make Homo Northwestus different from, say, a Tyke or a Midlander? What is he famous for now? And what, if anything, will hold him together for the future?

The place makes sense, at least. There is a logic to an area called the North-West which supercedes and surpasses even Lancashire as it was before the boundaries changed. More and more people give less and less thought to a day in the Lake District or a weekend in North Wales. They'll zoom out with their hiking boots and windsurfers from Timperley or Runcorn, but how often will they feel on foreign ground, as they might in York, or Stoke-on-Trent? Homo Northwestus feels he can belong now in Cumbria or Clywd and, increasingly, he uses the North-West as the phrase which delineates his patch.

It's a region with a distinct landscape, a bog guarded north and south by the mountains of Cumbria and Snowdonia; west and east by the Irish Sea and the bleakly beautiful Pennine chain. From Derbyshire up the spine of England was a poor land, and the tribes who clung to it were poor people until the last century put them on the map. And now, admit it, it is lovely to see what could not be seen thirty years ago. The hills have returned from the soot and grime which obliterated them, and the wilderness which had once held Homo Northwestus back is now his greatest asset. Regularly it's 'quality of life' which tops the list for people living here today and slowly, sometimes secretly, it seems most of the tribe is inching forwards. But not all.

It is sad, along places like Oldham Road in Manchester, to see how much has gone. Practically every other building was a pub or shop once. The Packhorse and the Playhouse Café. The Lancaster and The Royal Oak, where Thursday night talent contests would fill with every Sinatra soundalike Newton Heath could offer. Where once it was teeming with life it is boarded up and broken. A tree grows out of a shattered window and a spray-painted sign wishfully declares: 'Rave '90 Coming Soon'. For miles and miles, on both sides, are the gap-toothed, crumbling remains of an artery which flowed down with its oxygen from the mighty mill-towns of North-East Lancashire direct to the great cotton exchanges of Manchester.

> 6 Even by the 1920s the great manufacturing hive was in decline, with cotton jobs vanishing by the 100,000. 9

But was it ever so? Money has always buzzed around the North-West, creating greatness and power wherever it temporarily alighted. For the monks it was Furness and Furness Abbey. For the military of the Middle Ages it would be Lancaster Castle or Chester. For the maritime merchants it would be Liverpool. And, for just four generations, it had been Manchester; the seemingly invincible queen bee, with its loyal satellite towns full of workers. Bolton and Bury. Blackburn and Burnley. Oldham, Rochdale and Accrington. But even by the mid-'twenties the great manufacturing hive was in turmoil. In Lancashire 300,000 cotton jobs vanished between 1912 and 1937. In Greater Manchester 100,000 manufacturing jobs disappeared in the three bitter years which followed 1979. Today it's Cheshire which grows and, ever more, the shift of influence is to the south and west of the region.

Stand in Victoria Station and feel dwarfed by the scale of this change. From its famous platform – 2,194 feet long – freight and passengers would flow across a northern trading empire which bridged the New World with the old. On the huge painted station wall-map, the now-defunct rail links stand out like veins, each drawn in red across cream-coloured ceramic bricks. Every day seven hundred trains would pull onto one of Victoria's seventeen platforms, taking on and discharging 40,000 passengers. There was an overhead baggage railway which carried luggage to your platform, and on the stained glass entrance canopy the Lancashire and Yorkshire Railway promised you a quality journey, be it to Brussels or Blackpool. Today it's mostly commuters, and pre-packed bacon sandwiches, you'll find at Victoria, shuffling under the tracks and dodging the wrought iron tunnel supports – and that bustle of international commerce has moved south to where? To Manchester International Airport? By 2005 the terminals there could be handling thirty million passengers every year, and already it is Europe's fastest-growing airport.

Victoria Station. Lime Street in Liverpool. Ringway and Speke. The M61 and the M56. It was transport which knitted the North-West together, then as now. Homo Northwestus had given the world its first passenger station at Liverpool Road in Manchester, just as, later, he would provide Britain's first designated stretch of motorway around Preston. And once he'd cottoned up and cottoned on, the richest of the species welded old Lancashire to his beloved little empire of colonies. Up to the Lake District, down to the lawns of Prestbury and all along the North Welsh coast, it was Lancashire money which helped pay the 10,000 navvies who laid the track and built the 155 bridges from Lancaster to Carlisle in 1846. It was Lancashire money which flowed into North Wales after the Chester and Holyhead Railway opened for traffic on May 1st 1848, the first sod having been cut on St. David's Day three years before.

On the shingle shores of Llandudno and around mucky Liverpool bay, the old mucky money from the cotton trade set up its villas and bungalows. And if there wasn't a resort to suit him already, Homo Northwestus built one. The four trains which ran daily from Chester to Bangor in 1848 had nowhere to stop between Abergele and Conway until Manchester men (using Welsh builders) built themselves a resort and called it Colwyn Bay. Again, it was Homo Northwestus who pushed his empire around the West

▷ Victoria Station, Manchester . . . this was like Manchester International Airport once.

Cumbrian coast, hoping to develop Seascale as a grand bathing paradise. Ambitious plans were drawn up by the Furness Railway Company and by 1891 they could report 89 well-to-do families enjoying the sea and the newly-laid golf links of this pre-nuclear, sub-zero 'Eastbourne of the North'.

Few people go to Seascale now to take the waters. But the inherited lines of Victorian communications, fused with the natural shape of the region, have bound the North-West together. In Wales, where they have fought to retain an ancient identity, this might not be popular. But is not Rhyl the tribal homeland of Homo Northwestus as much as Bowness or Barrow-in-Furness? For 135 years the species has driven its railway cuttings, or tunnelled its rivers, and North Wales has been tied, tarmac and sleeper, to North-West England. One place certainly, but is Homo Northwestus one people?

Places like Abergele or Grange-over-Sands may hold a clue to the answer; retirement towns, where the great grandchildren of true Homo Northwestus, authentic Lancashire Man, measure out their days in coffee mornings and charity jumbles. Of both places it is said that people go there to die only to forget why they went, living on and feeling fitter than ever they did before. And it's from untroubled colonies like this that an older generation looks back on its patch with alarm and sees a new species with which he is not entirely in accord . . .

A member of the Abergele Gentlemen's Club sums the mood of general disillusionment with the Lancashire of today: 'I think that when you break up a community it takes a long, long while to re-establish that, because you've destroyed the essential soul and heart of what was a real, live community where everyone worked, lived and helped each other. Now it's self before anything and the idea of helping people in your community has largely disappeared.'

> 6 It is said that people go to Grange-over-Sands and Abergele to die, only to forget why they went. 9

Few of his Abergele chums would disagree and, to a man, they describe their old Lancashire stomping grounds as graffiti-grim places, in turns 'terrible', 'horrifying', and seemingly peppered with shops selling sexual appliances. As one they decry Manchester's Arndale Centre – who doesn't? – and mourn for a past supplanted by a colourless present and soulless future.

But if they're right, and if their North-West has disappeared, then what is replacing it is very interesting. It's suburban, it's modern, it's forward-looking and increasingly a better bet than the south.

Almost universally Homo Northwestus was a music hall joke, but now the tide is turned and the joke is no longer on him. It's true that parts of the region are still woefully badly off. In Manchester itself nearly half the working population receives less than two-thirds of average earnings. Homo Northwestus had been 38th out of 38. He'd climbed out of his bog and still his greatest industrial city is among the poorest in the land, with only Durham below it in the league. But drive out of these inner areas and you'll not find much the North-West is short of. Look at *Lancashire Life*, look at *Cheshire Life*; you'll not find much to choose between them. Everywhere really is the same as everywhere else, if you've got money.

△ Brewing up at the Abergele Gents Club. When one of the members is having a rough time of it, there are 160 pairs of sympathetic shoulders to lean on.

Homo Northwestus has caved in and has almost everything in his lifestyle he once despised the south for. How many eat tripe? Not as many as buy their fresh green chilli peppers in Sainsbury's. At places like Clitheroe Castle the species stood up (unsuccessfully) to the marauding Scots. Homo Northwestus planted his flag on the rough rock against William Fitzduncan and his Galloway gangsters back in June 1138. But today he's under pressure from bigger Macs with bigger bucks who see the North-West as just another part of their corporate, global strategy.

So has the independence Clitheroe Castle stood for all gone? Not entirely. There are pockets of resistance where the sounds of rattling sabres can still be heard. Drive up the East Lancs Road, or under the Wallasey Tunnel where 'Macdonalds welcomes you to Liverpool', and you'll find people still capable of taking a stand, making a fight of it. If the tabloid media are to be believed – and they're not – it's all they ever do on Merseyside.

▽ The Barton Bridge on the canal that Manchester merchants built to gain direct access to the sea and so · avoid the dock dues imposed by their Liverpool colleagues.

Liverpool has always been something else, Scousers a bit of a race apart. Although still old Lancashire's biggest city by population, it's felt by many not to belong, to be separated by history and temperament, always a bit eccentrically its own, only

half-Lancashire and Liverpudlians very, very special. Even when people thought old Lancashire was united, one people, there had been division. When you could assign one docker to every one bunch of African bananas there had been rivalry between Manchester and Liverpool, as between Edinburgh and Glasgow. The Ship Canal had been built in 1894, a 35-mile waterway just for Manchester merchants to avoid paying Liverpool dock fees. Its construction had been the stock in-joke of Liverpool's Victorian comics, but no-one laughed at the mutual antipathy the canal's success unleashed. No-one realised quite how thorny the Red Rose could become. And it's only now, a century later, that the storm has eased. Until Liverpool play Manchester United.

But if Scousers are a separate, measurable branch of the species Homo Northwestus, it isn't because of their accents. Until the first half of the last century they would have sounded much like people from Preston or Blackburn. It was the invading masses of Europe's first refugees, the Irish, whose intonations fused with the native dialect to create what we hear today. Always in the history of Liverpool it is its proximity to the sea which created the way Liverpudlians are. Few of the 300,000 Irish who washed up on the city between July 1847 and July 1848 ever intended to stay.

The West Prospect of the Town of LIVERPOOL as it appeared about the Year 1680

△ From humble beginnings Liverpool grew to dominate the world of shipping.

They'd come to catch ships to America, not to vanish into the city's already chronic slums. In 1842 the Cunard Line had opened a regular passenger service across the Atlantic. Trade routes were being driven towards India's cotton market and the great docks of Clarence, Waterloo, Victoria and Trafalgar were open and bustling with wealth.

In 1673 there had been only six streets in Liverpool. For commerce and industry it was dwarfed by Coventry and Norwich, Bristol and Exeter. One hundred years later there were 166 streets and Daniel Defoe was writing of 'One of the wonders of Britain. What it may grow in time, I know not'. And, like Topsy, it did grow. In 1848 the Stanley, Collingwood, Salisbury and Bramley Moore docks were opened and Liverpool's domination of North American trade was complete. More docks would follow at Bootle and Seaforth, completing a seven-mile haven where still, grey waters

housed ever-bigger sailing ships behind the granite sea wall.

But Liverpool wasn't the first place Homo Northwestus had chosen for his most important outlet to the sea. To the Romans it was Chester and Ravenglass. To the early slave and cotton traders it was Sunderland Point at the mouth of the Lune; or Lancaster itself, until silt drove the ships south to the Mersey and beyond. In this cycle of change a port would surely decline unless it could adapt, and Liverpool, for all its glory days, had no guaran-tees against the future. As for Victoria Station in Man-chester, so for the Albert Dock. As trading patterns shifted, Liverpool con-fronted a reality it was powerless to affect. Suddenly it was on the wrong side of the country. Just as before, when the great cathedrals of York and Lincoln were built, all the clever money suddenly appeared in the south and east.

Not that it ground to a halt entirely. Although the Mersey Docks and Har-bour Company employ under 500 dock workers today, compared with 14,000 in 1966, they'll proudly tell you how 40,000

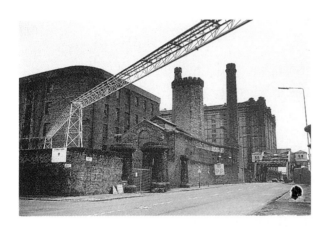

△ . . . all the clever money suddenly appeared in the south and east of England.

North-West jobs are supported by dock activity; how in 1990 over 23 million tonnes of cargo crossed the quays; and how Liverpool is still the major British port for trade with the eastern seaboard of the United States. Containers killed the jobs and aeroplanes killed the great Cunard liners, but so far the old images the world has of Liverpool simply refuse to lie down and die.

It's dereliction that people expect to see on Merseyside and, for all the stunning dockside rehabilitation schemes, there is still plenty of that. The Mersey Docks and Harbour Company point out that while Liverpool lost 250,000 man-days through strikes in 1972, it lost none in 1986. But you can't strike if you don't work, and more than anything it is the pattern of redundancy which has so embittered Merseysiders with memories. It's unlikely to be retired stevedores, they'll tell you, who snap up the four hundred luxury apartments in Barratt's redeveloped Waterloo Dock warehouse. And while the rest of Homo Northwestus has moved on and accepted the inevitable redundancy of cotton and coal, in Liverpool there's a much angrier reluctance to let go of the past. Or there seems to be. What to many on the Mersey is a determination not to let go of principles, not to go down without a fight is, to many others, no more than blinkered bloody-mindedness.

I n the single-storey extension of a Wallasey semi, Clive Garner is threading a film around the spools of his 16mm projector. Through the glass of the tiny projection room he can just make out the velvet seats of his own private cinema. Although there will be no ice lollies, the concealed red lights and the muted first clarinet of a forgotten dance band combine to put most astonished visitors at ease. This is possibly the smallest private cinema in Britain, and Clive's collection of Merseyside archive films is just as unique.

There are many which show Liverpool in its maritime pomp. Flunkeys load stickered portmanteaux onto hoists which sweep up and out, over the Pier Head and down onto the decks of great New York-bound liners. A couple embrace before the camera and are

◁ New Brighton . . . Cheshire's 'gay resort' of 1959.

lost for a moment in a cloud of fur. Weeping women in shawls gaze emptily at a billboard on the dock road. The *Titanic* has been reported lost and a city is in grief. Everywhere there are hordes of people erupting and spreading like spores from the ferries to the offices and sheds of a supremely confident maritime metropolis. And best of all is Clive's film, 'New Brighton, Cheshire's Gay Resort'.

There is no soundtrack on 'Cheshire's Gay Resort'. It was shot in flawless Kodacolour over thirty years ago and every frame is better than a paragraph of the purplest prose. In 1959 the River Mersey was not the polluted disgrace it is today, and at tide up on New Brighton beach there wasn't room to swing a biffbat, so popular was it then. Every ferry leaving the soot-stained Liver Buildings would be full of mothers in bright-checked gingham, dads combing back their hair, children clutching metal buckets and wooden-shafted spades. The smoky stack of a cargo ship might smudge the sky, but in 'Cheshire's Gay Resort' the sun is always shining. Every deckchair and donkey is occupied, and at Europe's largest outdoor swimming pool, Harry Secombe is kissing Miss New Brighton and plugging his summer show . . .

It's easy to understand how people might feel in Liverpool when you look at films like this. The city has lost so much, and not just in shipping. In the 'eighties there were hundreds of firms from Tate & Lyle to Meccano, which folded or fled. But, while some ceased trading altogether, there were others which seemed to be escaping the place or its name, rather than acting upon an economic impera-tive. They'd announce a restructuring plan, a rationalisation, and their business would re-group somewhere else, with regret. In Homo Northwestus 'Liverpudlius' the feeling grew that his share of the recession was the lion's share and when he elected politicians who roared, the media myth of the Liverpool bogeyman was born. Roll over Derek Hatton. Roll over George Formby.

However hard you promote the truth, there are few things more difficult to escape from than a pigeonhole. No sooner had he shed the Formby-Lowry skin than Homo Northwestus (Liverpool chapter) was lumped in with Militant. The aggressive, hectoring style of the Hatton era, with its direct challenging of government, made fertile copy and lively, confrontational pictures. It so dominated wider perceptions of Liverpool that, says historian John Walton, 'the instant coverage of the new mass media is so selective and distorted as to give most people little more real understanding than was available, more slowly and tortuously, to Elizabeth I's governments'.

'The Lancashire which is presented on the national stage,' he writes, 'is largely a matter of the doings of football teams in Manchester and Liverpool, and the allegedly subversive activities of the "revolutionary" left in the financially beleaguered Merseyside metropolis.' But it wasn't all fiction. Derek Hatton and Tony Mulhearne did not march to the Town Hall alone. Despite their lack of presentational *finesse*, didn't they truly give voice to a city's anger and frustration?

Ask a Scouser; see what he or she says. Not one hundred yards from Gambier Terrace (where the young John Lennon had his flat) is the lock-up where Don Griffiths plies his trade. He's a self-employed mechanic and when Don first started up his workshop, The Beatles hadn't even written 'Sgt. Pepper's'. The M.P. for Huyton was Prime Minister, and Liverpool was synonymous with success. Nothing's bubbling much now though – unless you count the paint-splattered kettle – and Don's as likely to be stripping his wife's Metro as a client's carburettor. 'It's dead right now,' says Don, 'Absolutely dead.'

It's never completely silent, however. Around the stove which Don feeds with drained sump oil, gather the wise and the worldly. From polytechnic lecturers to part-time painters, they'll pop in to wrestle with the national debt or Third World famine in the time it takes to sink a brew.

'The thing about Liverpool,' says Don, warming to his second favourite subject (his first being an old Liverpool 'nobby' boat he's restored), 'the thing about Liverpool is that there are no grey areas. We have no qualms about saying, "that's a nice car, how much did it cost you?' or "how much do you earn".' Why? 'We've had so many people coming and going, so much unemployment, and that makes you more upfront.'

'And don't forget, Liverpool was Tory council once. Liverpool, Tory! So the city has changed politically and we're strong Labour now. But if the people who voted Conservative then are voting Labour now, something must have changed. Maybe people do think we've had a bad deal. Maybe it's not justified but people do think that way.'

He'll stick up and speak up for what he believes is right, will Homo Northwestus 'Liverpudlius'. 'We cling on to our values, we look after our own,' says Don. Unlike the rest of the species,

△ 'The thing about Liverpool,' says mechanic Don Griffiths, 'is there are no grey areas.'

Liverpool Man has looked outwards to the sea and grown vocal in support of his singular way of life. If Don's analysis is right, it's for saying what others are thinking that the Scouser's card has been marked.

Now it will be the image-makers whose job it is to play Canute and turn the tide on the city's poor PR. This year they'll be taking off to the United States. They'll leapfrog Liverpool's tabloid tormentors and blow their trumpets before American investors who can only remember a city synonymous with success . . . when The Beatles wrote 'Sgt. Pepper's' . . . when the MP for Huyton was Prime Minister . . .

All of Lancashire has suffered, not just Liverpool, and unemployment matters have often been much worse in the cotton towns. The county had been a self-sufficient domain, almost an independent state, with an intricate, industrious economy whose parts made a whole. Although Liverpool and Manchester might bicker, their prospects were tightly bound together. When cotton slumped in the 1920s the domino effect could be felt in both cities and throughout the region. Lancashire employers had failed to match the technological advances of their rival cotton countries. In Japan, India, Italy and, ironically, the United States, cheaper fabrics were being produced, often by cheaper labour. Suddenly, and staggeringly, Homo Northwestus found that the game he had invented was being played much better by someone else.

> 6 Suddenly Homo Northwestus found that the game he'd invented was being played much better by someone else. 9

When cotton suffered, so did engineering. When engineering suffered, so did the coal industry, with 40,000 leaving the pits between 1923 and 1937. In this climate it was no surprise that Liverpool would suffer too. Both imports and exports of cotton fell, with direct consequences for dock labour as well as the many service companies whose future depended on a successful port. Southampton overtook Liverpool as Britain's top passenger terminal, and the days of the liners, the symbol of Liverpool's greatness, were numbered.

Suddenly, Homo Northwestus was contemplating the bog again. In less than a hundred years he'd climbed to the top and shaken off his narrow, neglected past. But when his chosen industry had turned out to be about as stable as the Pennine peat, what could he do? What is Homo Northwestus famous for now? Work, and the way he worked, had forged a character and a way of life that was uniquely his. For his graft he'd been noted, but suddenly the old patterns of work could no longer sustain the image. So what is the tribe famous for now? During the filming of the documentaries, this was a question Ray Gosling asked every one of our interviewees. No two answers were the same . . .

'Tourism is the growth industry of Lancashire' – Jim Atherton.

'It's very, very sad to say, but it's not famous for very many things now, but it's still got grit and determination, and some lovely country' – Benny Rothman, rambler.

'I think we breed harder footballers up here . . . In the England team of the 'fifties they always came up north for the players. One or two came from the south. But not many' – Tom Finney.

'I don't think, to be honest, it's very famous for anything very much now' – Mark Whitlock-Blundell.

'There's an awful lot of small businesses . . . the insides of fountain pens are made at Blackburn' – Simon Towneley.

'Nothing' – Mani Passerini.

'Football teams, aren't we? Or famous for being very pleasant people, perhaps' – Tony Harrison.

'The North-West has turned into a gigantic museum, a vast area of ancient industrial landscape' – John Smith, historian.

Everything. That's what Homo Northwestus is famous for now. From windowless warehouses he'll supply the world with plastic litter bins, greetings cards, vinyl wall coverings, brake linings, tubular bandages, toilet rolls and machines for making cigarettes. Even as the cotton withered on the stem, Trafford Park (the world's first industrial estate) was showing a new way for smaller, more diverse industries which often needed only transport and storage to flourish and grow. Increasingly now, Homo Northwestus stacked his new workplace along the edge of the hard shoulder. In new towns and on industrial parks, he created a motorway culture and once again it seemed the shift was southwards within his patch.

> **6 Homo Northwestus was changing, not declining. He was learning to adapt. 9**

Homo Northwestus was changing, not declining. He was learning to adapt much better than his ancestors had when cotton first threatened his peaceful backwater; when he rioted and resented all new ideas. Homo Northwestus was becoming a thoroughly modern man. Roll over, George Formby. Mike Harding, fill your pipe up. Here was a message of defiance; not defensive, not apologising. It wasn't the old Lancashire of Abergele gentlemen. It wasn't a community with an 'essential soul'. It was more a collection of individual spirits, but it was turning the corner – even if Homo Northwestus did not universally approve of what he saw there.

On the outskirts of his towns, leisure parks sprang up on previously bleak wastelands. Places like Pilsworth, south of Bury, where consumers can shop at Asda, eat a deep-pan pizza, watch a movie, or sip coke to the rumble of runaway bowls, all within a trolley-push of the same giant carpark. Cotton resurfaced – sanitised and romanticised – in heritage centres or museums; and although it was never really here, Camelot has done ever so well off the M6 near Chorley, just as the cowboys are doing at Frontierland in Morecambe.

But however nostalgic Homo Northwestus is for the good things of old Lancashire, it could be a dark and dispiriting place to live. At Megabowl's multi-lane bowling alleys they'll hire you flat-soled sneakers to protect their parquet strip, but it wasn't as much fun in Oldham in 1928 when 10,527 pairs of clogs were handed to needy children in just one month of a town's despair. Homo Northwestus likes it now. He might bemoan the coming of America to his malls and estates, but at least and at last he's got what everybody else has got: the self-same retail warehouse franchised outlets here as in Milton Keynes . . .

For so long Homo Northwestus had been stammering and apologising, having a fool for his hero. He'd been 38th out of 38. The Bronze Age had all but passed him by. Conan Doyle taunted him, saying the entire tribe was thick, higher in brawn that it could ever be in achievement. But now look. On John Dalton Street in Manchester the magnificent façade of a Victorian office has been saved. Sturdy steel legs have held it secure – a slice of window and stone – until a 21st-century office development behind it is completed. It's the best of what Homo Northwestus was, being used as a shop window for what he is today . . .

There are a few battered relics of the past untouched. Just outside Bacup, on the Todmorden Road, is a place where you could happily believe that Macdonalds or Megabowl had

△ The Britannia Coconutters of Bacup, complete with blackened faces and clogs. A bizarre mixture of traditional Lancashire and other (unidentified) cultural influences. A relic of the past . . .?

◁   The eccentric
muddle of curios and
contraptions which is
the pride and joy of
Bacup Natural History
Society.

never happened. There are mangles and miners' lamps, clogs and
clocking-on-clocks. There's a Ewbank, a football rattle, innumer-
able fire extinguishers, a stuffed seal, dozens of stuffed birds, Dinky
toys, Instamatic cameras and a row of manually-operated mincers.
In a long-abandoned pub, the Bacup Natural History Society has
set up its headquarters, and their eccentric muddle of curios and
contraptions now clutters an upstairs room which by arrangement
you can visit and enjoy.

Among the trays of butterflies and eggs you'll find a dehydrated
rat, the traps of a trapdoor spider, a collection of black and white

snaps from the Leica of a German tank commander and, just occasionally, a present-day member wondering why anyone would want to collect either lightbulbs or electric plugs. There is no commercial side to the Bacup Natural History Society. Its 120 members pay only £3 a year annual subscription and remain as dedicted to the preservation of Lancashire's fabric as the working-class naturalists who founded the movement in 1878.

In their precious spare time these pioneers had built up this collection and become more attached to their homeland than maybe Homo Northwestus can ever be again. They tramped it; they measured it; they lovingly collected and collated it; and they never left it.

Everyone wants to belong, to feel rooted, but as the old boundaries mean less to ever more of us, new loyalties are found. Loyalties to family or football club are much stronger than loyalty to the old county, and doesn't Lancashire exist now mainly as an idea? A thought to be kept in cupboards? A curiosity? Something to be dusted down, proudly held, perennially precious? Warmth and cotton and cobbles?

So is there any growing sense of belonging to the North-West? Not yet; not in that old Lancashire way. Too many of the tribe are new – just as the Irish, the Scots and the Welsh nearly two centuries ago – and no-one can tell quite what bonding will occur. But some say that Homo Northwestus is now like a dozing giant, listening with glee to how the South-East gets itself knotted on its M25 . . . and waiting for his moment to burst its genius on a world it has already changed once.

Homo Northwestus will never be nothing again.

Roll over George Formby.

Recommended further reading

Paul Agnew, *Finney – a football legend* (Carnegie Publishing).
Peter Aughton, *Liverpool – A People's History* (Carnegie Publishing).
J. J. Bagley, *The Earls of Derby* (Sidgewick & Jackson).
Bob Dobson (ed.), *From Lancashire Lips – dialect verse* (Landy Publishing).
Kathleen Eyre, *The Real Lancashire* (Dalesman).
P. Gooderson, *A History of Lancashire* (Batsford).
Nick Higham, *The Northern Counties to AD 1000* (Longman).
Brian Hollingworth, 'The Centenary of Edwin Waugh's Death', *Journal of the Lancashire Dialect Society,* No. xxxix.
John Kennedy, *The Clifton Chronicle* (Carnegie Publishing,).
J. Marshall and J. K. Walton, *The Lake Counties* (Manchester University Press).
Benita Moore, *Lancashire Lives* Vols. 1 and 2 (Carnegie Publishing).
Roy Millward, *Lancashire* (Hodder & Stoughton).
William Murphy, *The Father of the Submarine* (William Kimber).
Frank Musgrove, *The North of England* (Blackwell).
Frank Neal, *Sectarian Violence – The Liverpool Experience* (M.U.P.).
Jeff Nuttall, *King Twist: A Portrait of Frank Randle* (Routledge).
Keith Parry, *The Resorts of the Lancashire Coast* (David & Charles).
Arthur Redford, *Labour Migration in England* (M.U.P.).
John Martin Robinson, *A Guide to the Country Houses of the North-West* (Constable).
Paul Salveson, *The People's Monuments* (Workers' Educational Association).
John Singleton, *Lancashire on the Scrapheap* (Oxford).
J. K. Walton, *Lancashire, a social history 1558–1939* (M.U.P.).

Note on the illustrations

Except for those listed hereafter all of the original photographs in this book were taken by Ian Beesley, to whom we are extremely grateful. Granada Television kindly provided the photographs on pages 2, 3, 37, 40, 44, 62, 88 and 99. The reproduction of the painting on page 7 is by kind permission of the Botanic Gardens Museum, Southport. The photograph of the Poulton Elk on page 10 is by Anna Goddard and is reproduced by kind permission of the Harris Museum and Art Gallery, Preston. The photographs of the Roman coins on page 18 and of the Wigan Pit Brow Girls on page 9 are reproduced by permission of John Hannavy Picture Collection, Wigan. The photograph of Hardknott Fort on page 18 is by Alistair Hodge, as are the photographs of Miles Gerard on page 24 (which are reproduced by kind permission of Rev. Fr. T. K. Hodson of St. Robert's Church, Catforth), and the photographs on pages 25 and 90. The photograph of Bill Shankly on page 33 is reproduced by permission of the *Liverpool Echo.* The engraving on page 35 is from the *Illustrated London News.* The photograph of Lord Leverhulme is reproduced by permission of Unilever. The photograph of the *Resurgam* on page 76 is reproduced by permission of William Murphy. The photograph of the Pankhursts on page 80 is reproduced by kind permission of the Lancashire Library. The engraving of the original Lathom House is taken from Draper's *House of Stanley* (1864). The engraving of Liverpool in 1680 on page 114 is reproduced by kind permission of Liverpool Central Libraries. Our thanks to all these people and institutions.